THE INNER REACHES OF
OUTER SPACE

JOSEPH CAMPBELL

THE INNER REACHES
OF OUTER SPACE

METAPHOR AS MYTH AND AS RELIGION

JOSEPH CAMPBELL
FOUNDATION

New World Library
Novato, California

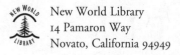

New World Library
14 Pamaron Way
Novato, California 94949

Cover design: Mary Ann Casler
Type design: Tona Pearce Myers

Library of Congress Cataloging-in-Publication Data

Campbell, Joseph, 1904–1987
The inner reaches of outer space : metaphor as myth and as religion /
Joseph Campbell.
    p.   cm.
Originally published: New York : A. van der Marck, ©1986.
Includes bibliographical references and index.
ISBN 978-1-57731-209-3 (alk. paper)
1. Mythology. 2. Religion. 3. Metaphor—Religious aspects. I. Title.
BL311 .C263 2002
291.1´3—dc21   2001005890

First paperback printing, July 2012
ISBN 978-1-60868-110-5
Printed in Canada on 100% postconsumer-waste recycled paper

New World Library is proud to be a Gold Certified Environmentally Responsible Publisher. Publisher certification awarded by Green Press Initiative. www.greenpressinitiative.org

10 9 8 7 6 5 4 3 2 1

For
Barbara, Jean, and Lynne

CONTENTS

ABOUT THE COLLECTED WORKS OF
JOSEPH CAMPBELL

At his death in 1987, Joseph Campbell left a significant body of published work that explored his lifelong passion, the complex of universal myths and symbols that he called "Mankind's one great story." He also left, however, a large volume of unreleased work: uncollected articles, notes, letters, and diaries, as well as audio- and videotape recorded lectures.

The Joseph Campbell Foundation was founded in 1991 to preserve, protect, and perpetuate Campbell's work. The Foundation has undertaken to archive his papers and recordings in digital format, and to publish previously unavailable material and out-of-print works as *The Collected Works of Joseph Campbell.*

THE COLLECTED WORKS OF JOSEPH CAMPBELL
Robert Walter, Executive Editor
David Kudler, Managing Editor

FOREWORD

The chapters of this volume have been developed from lectures delivered in San Francisco, 1981–1984, to themes proposed by Barbara McClintock, Director of Public Programs at the C. G. Jung Institute in that city, and by Lynne Kaufman, Program Director, International Studies, at the University of California, Berkeley. *The Inner Reaches of Outer Space* was the title and topic of a symposium organized by Barbara McClintock in 1983, where, before an immense audience brought together in the great hall of The Palace of Fine Arts, I shared the platform with the astronaut Rusty Schweickart. *Metaphor As Myth and As Religion* was the title of my address delivered in 1984, also in that great hall, at the festival instituted by Lynne Kaufman in celebration of my eightieth birthday. The poet Robert Bly, archaeologist Marija Gimbutas, tai chi master Al Chungliang Huang, philosopher Sam Keen, psychologist Stanley Keleman, and anthropologist Barbara Meyerhoff shared the platform on that spectacular occasion, which terminated with a descent from the high ceiling of a galaxy of balloons. To my wife, Jean Erdman, dancer and choreographer, I owe the whole theme and argument of my lecture "The Way of Art," composed in 1981 for Barbara McClintock's symposium, *A Call to Beauty*, conducted by James Hillman; while my talk on "Myth and the Body" was introductory to an all-day seminar on mythology as a function of biology, held in 1982 at the C. G. Jung Institute.

My desire and great pleasure in the preparation of this little volume has been as rendering a return gift to the Graces for the transforming insights of these recent years, which, with the cooperation of their wonderfully willing San Francisco audiences, we have been testing out in a broadly shared spiritual adventure.

—Joseph Campbell

MYTH AND THE BODY

Reviewing with unprejudiced eye the religious traditions of mankind, one becomes very soon aware of certain mythic motifs that are common to all, though differently understood and developed in the differing traditions: ideas, for example, of a life beyond death, or of malevolent and protective spirits. Adolf Bastian (1826–1905), a medical man, world traveler, and leading ethnologist of the nineteenth century, for whom the chair in anthropology at the University of Berlin was established, termed these recurrent themes and features "elementary ideas," *Elementargedanken,* designating as "ethnic" or "folk ideas," *Völkergedanken,* the differing manners of their representation, interpretation, and application in the arts and customs, mythologies and theologies, of the peoples of this single planet.

Such a recognition of two aspects, a universal and a local, in the constitution of religions everywhere clarifies at one stroke those controversies touching eternal and temporal values, truth and falsehood, which forever engage theologians; besides setting apart, as of two distinct yet related sciences, studies on the one hand of the differing "ethnic" or "folk ideas," which are the concern properly of historians and ethnologists, and on the other hand, of the *Elementargedanken,* which pertain to psychology. A number of leading psychologists of the past century addressed themselves to the analysis of these universals, of whom Carl G. Jung (1875–1961), it seems to me, was the most insightful and illuminating. The same mythic motifs that Bastian had termed "elementary ideas," Jung called "archetypes of the collective unconscious," transferring emphasis, thereby, from the mental sphere of rational ideation to the obscure subliminal abysm out of which dreams arise.

For myths and dreams, in this view, are motivated from a single psychophysiological source—namely, the human imagination moved by the conflicting urgencies of the organs (including the brain) of the human body, of which the anatomy has remained pretty much the same since c. 40,000 B.C. Accordingly, as the imagery of a dream is metaphorical of the psychology of its dreamer, that of a mythology is metaphorical of the psychological posture of the people to whom it pertains. The sociological structure coordinate to such a posture was termed by the Africanist Leo Frobenius (1873–1938) a cultural "monad." Every feature of such a social organism is, in his sense, expressive and therefore symbolic of the informing psychological posture. In *The Decline of the West*, Oswald Spengler (1880–1936) identified eight colossal monads of great majesty, with a ninth now in formation, as having shaped and dominated world history since the rise, in the fourth millennium B.C., of the first literate high cultures —(1) the Sumero-Babylonian, (2) the Egyptian, (3) the Greco-Roman (Apollonian), (4) the Vedic-Aryan, of India, (5) the Chinese, (6) the Maya-Aztec-Incan, (7) the Magian (Persian-Arabian, Judeo-Christian-Islamic), (8) the Faustian (Gothic-Christian to modern European-American), and now, beneath the imposed alien crust of a Marxian cultural pseudomorphosis, (9) the germinating Russian-Christian.[1]

Long antecedent, however, to the world-historical appearances, flowerings, and inevitable declines of these monumental monads, an all but timeless period is recognized of nonliterate, aboriginal societies—some nomadic hunters, others settled horticulturalists; some of no more than a half dozen related families, others of tens of thousands. And each had its mythology—some, pitifully fragmentary, but others, marvelously rich and magnificently composed. These mythologies were all conditioned, of course, by local geography and social necessities. Their images were derived from the local landscapes, flora and fauna, from recollections of personages and events, shared visionary experiences, and so forth. Narrative themes and other mythic features, furthermore, have passed from one domain to another. However, the definition of the "monad" is not a function of the number and character of such influences and details, but of the psychological stance in relation to their universe of the people, whether great or small, of whom the monad is the cohering life. The study of any mythology from the point of view of an ethnologist or historian, therefore, is of the relevance of its metaphors to a disclosure of the structure and force of the nucleating monad by which every feature of the culture is invested with its spiritual sense. Out of this emerge the forms of its art, its tools, and its weapons, ritual forms, musical instruments, social regulations, and ways of relating in war and in peace to its neighbors.

In terms of Bastian's vocabulary, these monads are local organizations of the number of "ethnic" or "folk ideas" of the represented cultures, constellating variously in relation to current needs and interests the primal energies and urges of the common human species: bioenergies that are of the essence of life itself, and which, when unbridled, become terrific, horrifying, and destructive.

The first, most elementary and horrifying of all, is the innocent voraciousness of life, which feeds on lives and provides the first interest of the infant feeding on its mother. The peace of sleep shatters in nightmare into apparitions of the cannibal ogress, cannibal giant, or approaching crocodile, which are features, also, of the fairy tale. In Dionysiac orgies the culminating frenzies issue still, in some parts of the world, in the merciless group-cannibalizing of living bulls. The most telling mythological image of this grim first premise of life is to be seen in the Hindu figure of the worldmother herself as Kālī, "Black Time," licking up with her extended, long, red tongue the lives of all the living of this world of her creation. For, as noticed in a paper on ritual killing by Adolf E. Jensen, the late director of the Frobenius Institute in Frankfurt-am-Main, "It is the common mark of all animal life that it can maintain itself only by destroying life;" citing to this point an Abyssinian song in celebration of the joys of life: "He who has not yet killed, shall kill. She who has not yet given birth shall bear."[2]

The second primal compulsion, linked almost in identity with the first (as recognized in this Abyssinian paean), is the sexual, generative urge, which during the years of passage out of infancy comes to knowledge with such urgency that in its seasons it overleaps the claims even of the first. For here the species talks. The individual is surpassed. In the quiver of the Hindu god Kāma, whose name means "desire" and "longing," and who is a counterpart of Cupid—no child, however, but a splendid youth, emitting a fragrance of blossoms, dark and magnificent as an elephant stung with vehement desire—there are five flowered arrows to be sent flying from his flowery bow, and their names are "Open Up!" "Exciter of the Paroxysm of Desire," "The Inflamer," "The Parcher," and "The Carrier of Death." Orgies of whole companies overtaken by the released zeal of the arrows of this god are reported from every quarter of the globe.

A third motivation, which has been the unique generator of the action on the stage of world history—since the period, at least, of Sargon I of Akkad, in southern Mesopotamia, c. 2300 B.C.—is the apparently irresistible impulse to plunder. Psychologically, this might perhaps be read as an extension of the bioenergetic command to feed upon and consume; however, the motivation here is not of any such primal biological urgency, but of an impulse launched from the eyes, not to consume, but to possess. An ample anthology of exemplary texts to this purpose, readily at hand, will be found in the Bible; for example:

> When the Lord your God brings you into the land which you are entering to take possession of it, and clears away many nations before you, the Hittites, the Girgashites, the Amorites, the Canaanites, the Perizzites, the Hivites, and the Jebusites, seven nations greater and mightier than yourselves, and when the Lord your God gives them over to you, and you defeat them; then you must utterly destroy them; you shall make no covenant with them and show them no mercy. You shall not make marriages with them, giving your daughters to their sons or taking their daughters for your sons. For they would turn away your sons from following me, to serve other gods; then the anger of the Lord would be kindled against you, and he would destroy you utterly. But thus shall you deal with them; you shall break down their altars, and dash in pieces their pillars, and hew down their Asherim, and burn their graven images with fire. For you are a people holy to the Lord your God; the Lord your God has chosen you to be a people for his

own possession, out of all the peoples that are on the face of the earth. (Deuteronomy 7:1–6)

When you draw near to a city to fight against it, offer terms of peace to it. And if its answer to you is peace and it opens to you, then all the people who are found in it shall do forced labor for you and shall serve you. But if it makes no peace with you, but makes war against you, then you shall besiege it; and when the Lord your God gives it into your hand you shall put all its males to the sword, but the women and the little ones, the cattle, and everything else in the city, all its spoil, you shall take as booty for yourselves; and you shall enjoy the spoil of your enemies, which the Lord your God has given you. Thus you shall do to all the cities which are very far from you, which are not cities of the nations here. But in the cities of these people that the Lord your God gives you for an inheritance, you shall save alive nothing that breathes, but you shall utterly destroy them, the Hittites and the Amorites, the Canaanites and the Perizzites, the Hivites and the Jebusites, as the Lord your God has commanded. (Deuteronomy 20:10–18)

And when the Lord your God brings you into the land which he swore to your fathers, to Abraham, to Isaac, and to Jacob, to give you, with great and goodly cities, which you did not build, and houses full of all good things, which you did not fill, and cisterns hewn out, which you did not hew, and vineyards and olive trees, which you did not plant, and when you eat and are full, then take heed lest you forget the Lord, who brought you out of the land of Egypt, out of the house of bondage. (Deuteronomy 6:10–12)

War gods of this kind, always tribal in their ranges both of mercy and of power, have abounded over the earth as the fomenting agents of world history. Indra of the Vedic Aryans, Zeus and Ares of the Homeric Greeks, were deities of this class, contemporary with Yahweh; and in the period (sixteenth to twentieth centuries A.D.) of the Spanish, Portuguese, French, and Anglo-Saxon struggles for hegemony over the peoples of the planet, even Christ, his saints, and the Virgin Mary were converted into the tutelaries of pillaging armies.

In the *Artha Śāstra,* "Textbook on the Art of Winning," which is a classic Indian treatise on polity believed to have been compiled by Kauṭilya, the counselor to the founder of the Maurya dynasty, King Chandragupta I (reigned c. 321–297 B.C.), the moral order by which all life is governed, and according to which kings and princes are therefore to be advised, is recognized and expounded as the "Law of the Fish" *(matsya-nyāya)*, which is, simply: "The big ones eat the little ones and the little ones have to be numerous and fast."

For, whether in the depths of the forgotten sea out of which life originated, or in the jungle of its evolution on land, or now in these great cities that are being built to be demolished in our recurrent wars, the same dread triad of god-given urgencies, of feeding, procreating, and overcoming, are the motivating powers. And for the proper functioning of at least the first and third of these motivations in the fish pond of world history, the first requirement in the order of nature—as already recognized in the passage just quoted from Deuteronomy 7:1–6 (seventh century B.C.)—is suppression of the natural impulse to mercy.

For the quality of mercy, empathy, or compassion is also a gift of nature, late to appear in the evolution of species, yet evident already in the play and care of their young of the higher mammals. In contrast to the bioenergetic urge to procreate, however, which is an immediate urgency of the organs, compassion, like the will to plunder, is an impulse launched from the eyes. Moreover, it is not tribal- or species-oriented, but open to the appeal of the whole range of living beings. So that one of the first concerns of the elders, prophets, and established priesthoods of tribal or institutionally oriented mythological systems has always been to limit and define the permitted field of expression of this expansive faculty of the heart, holding it to a fixed focus within the field exclusively of the ethnic monad, while deliberately directing outward every impulse to violence. Within the monadic horizon deeds of violence are forbidden: "Thou shalt not kill... Thou shalt not covet thy neighbor's wife" (Exodus 20:13, 17; also, Deuteronomy 5:17, 21), whereas abroad, such acts are required: "You shall put all its males to the sword, but the women... you shall take as booty to yourselves" (Deuteronomy 20:13–14). In Islamic thought the nations of the earth are distinguished as of two realms: *dar al'islām,* "the realm of submission [to Allah]," and *dar al'harb,* "the realm of war," which is to say, the rest of the world. And in

Christian thought, the words reported of the resurrected Christ to his eleven remaining apostles—"Go ye therefore, and make disciples of all the nations" (Matthew 28:19)—have been interpreted as a divine mandate for a conquest of the planet.

In our present day, when this same planet, Earth, rocking slowly on its axis in its course around the sun, is about to pass out of astrological range of the zodiacal sign of the Fish (Pisces) into that of the Water Bearer (Aquarius), it does indeed seem that a fundamental transformation of the historical conditions of its inhabiting humanity is in prospect, and that the age of the conquering armies of the contending monster monads— which was inaugurated in the time of Sargon I of Akkad, some 4,320 years ago, in southern Iraq—may be about to close.

For there are no more intact monadic horizons: all are dissolving. And along with them, the psychological hold is weakening of the mythological images and related social rituals by which they were supported. As already recognized half a century ago by the Irish poet Yeats in his foreboding vision "The Second Coming":

> Turning and turning in the widening gyre
> The falcon cannot hear the falconer;
> Things fall apart; the center cannot hold;
> Mere anarchy is loosed upon the world,
> The blood-dimmed tide is loosed, and everywhere
> The ceremony of innocence is drowned;
> The best lack all conviction, while the worst
> Are full of passionate intensity,
> Surely some revelation is at hand...[3]

The old gods are dead or dying and people everywhere are searching, asking: What is the new mythology to be, the mythology of this unified earth as of one harmonious being?

One cannot predict the next mythology any more than one can predict tonight's dream; for a mythology is not an ideology. It is not something projected from the brain, but something experienced from the heart, from recognitions of identities behind or within the appearances of nature, perceiving with love a "thou" where there would have been otherwise only an "it." As stated already centuries ago in the Indian Kena Upaniṣad (Upanishad): "That which in the lightning flashes forth, makes one blink, and say 'Ah!'—that 'Ah!' refers to divinity."[4] And centuries before that, in the Chhāndogya Upaniṣad (c. ninth century B.C.):

> When [in the world] one sees nothing else, hears nothing else, recog-nizes nothing else: that is [participation in] the Infinite. But when one sees, hears, and recognizes only otherness: that is smallness. The Infinite is the immortal. That which is small is mortal.
>
> But sir, that Infinite: upon what is it established?
>
> Upon its own greatness—or rather, not upon greatness. For by greatness people here understand cows and horses, elephants and gold, slaves, wives, mansions and estates. That is not what I mean; not that! For in that context everything is established on something else.
>
> This Infinite of which I speak is below. It is above. It is to the west, to the east, to the south, to the north. It is, in fact, this whole world. And accordingly, with respect to the notion of ego *(ahaṃkārādeśa):* I also am below, above, to the east, to the south, and to the north. I, also, am this whole world.
>
> Or again, with respect to the Self *(ātman):* The Self (the Spirit) is below, above, to the west, to the east, to the south, and to the north. The Self (the Spirit), indeed, is the whole world.
>
> Verily, the one who sees this way, thinks and understands this way, takes pleasure in the Self, delights in the Self, dwells with the Self and knows bliss in the Self; such a one is autonomous *(svarāj)*, mov-ing through all the world at pleasure *(kāmacāra)*. Whereas those who think otherwise are ruled by others *(anya-rājan)*, know but perishable pleasures, and are moved about the world against their will *(akā-macāra)*.[5]

The life of a mythology derives from the vitality of its symbols as metaphors delivering, not simply the idea, but a sense of actual participa-tion in such a realization of transcendence, infinity, and abundance, as this of which the upanishadic authors tell. Indeed, the first and most essential service of a mythology is this one, of opening the mind and heart to the utter wonder of all being. And the second service, then, is cosmological: of representing the universe and whole spectacle of nature, both as known to the mind and as beheld by the eye, as an epiphany of such kind that when lightning flashes, or a setting sun ignites the sky, or a deer is seen standing alerted, the exclamation "Ah!" may be uttered as a recognition of divinity.

This suggests that in the new mythology, which is to be of the whole human race, the old Near Eastern desacralization of nature by way of a doctrine of the Fall will have been rejected; so that any such limiting sentiment as that expressed in 2 Kings 5:15, "there is no God in all the earth but in Israel," will be (to use a biblical term) an abomination. The image of the universe will no longer be the old Sumero-Babylonian, locally centered, three-layered affair, of a heaven above and abyss below, with an ocean-encircled bit of earth between; nor the later, Ptolemaic one, of a mysteriously suspended globe enclosed in an orderly complex of revolving crystalline spheres; nor even the recent heliocentric image of a single planetary system at large within a galaxy of exploding stars; but (as of today, at least) an inconceivable immensity of galaxies, clusters of galaxies, and clusters of clusters (superclusters) of galaxies, speeding apart into expanding distance, with humanity as a kind of recently developed scurf on the epidermis of one of the lesser satellites of a minor star in the outer arm of an average galaxy, amidst one of the lesser clusters among the thousands, catapulting apart, which took form some fifteen billion years ago as a consequence of an inconceivable preternatural event. In chapter 1, the relevance to mythology of our present knowledge of this still-unfolding wonder is ventilated.

Chapter 2, which treats of the art of reading the pictorial script and interpreting the metaphorical vocabularies of mythology, is intended simply as a reminder of what we already know but tend to forget, which is that the historically conditioned forms of thought and language by which our lives are shaped are indeed historically conditioned, whereas the psychosomatic entity that is everywhere being shaped—namely, the bioenergetic system of the one species, *Homo sapiens sapiens*—is and has been for some forty millennia a constant. Hence, the "elementary ideas" (Bastian), or "archetypes of the collective unconscious" (Jung), of this single species—which are biologically grounded and at once the motivating powers and connoted references of the historically conditioned metaphorical figures of mythologies throughout the world—are, like the laws of space, unchanged by changes of location.

The new mythology, therefore, which is rapidly becoming a social as well as spiritual necessity as the monadic structures of the past dissolve, is already implicit among us as knowledge *a priori,* native to the mind. Its images, recognized with rapture as radiant of that greatness which is below, above, to the west, to the east, to the south, and to the north of this whole new universe and of all things, will be derived from contemporary life, thought, and experience, anywhere and everywhere, and the moral order to the support of which they are to be brought shall be of the monad of mankind.

In chapter 3, "The Way of Art," the radical transformation of mind and therewith of vision that is required for the recognition of all things in this way, as epiphanies of the rapture of being, is defined and discussed in terms of the principles of esthetics. For it is the artist who brings the images of a mythology to manifestation, and without images (whether mental or visual) there is no mythology. Moreover, it is the nonjudgmental way of seeing that is proper to the arts which allows things to stand forth and be seen simply as they are, as neither desirable nor to be feared, but as statements, each in its own mode, of the nature of being. In the words of William Blake: "If the doors of perception were cleansed, every thing would appear to man as it is, infinite." [6]

Thus viewed, in the way of the method of art, the features of an environment become transparent to transcendence, which is the way of vision of myth. Features of especial moment and objects of essential use acquire in this way symbolic significance, as do likewise personages in social roles of importance. The whole known world is thus experienced as an esthetic wonder. Its animals, rocks, and trees are the features of a Holy Land, radiant of eternity. Shrines are established, here and there, as sites of especial force or history. Certain birds and beasts are recognized as symbolically outstanding. And the social order is brought, as far as possible, to accord with an intuited order of nature, the whole sense of which is harmony and well-being.

Every functioning mythology is an organization of insights of this order, made known by way of works of visual art and verbal narrative (whether scriptural or oral) and applied to communal life by way of a calendar of symbolic rites, festivals, and manners, social classifications, pedagogic initiations, and ceremonies of investiture, by virtue of which the community is itself mythologized, to become metaphorical of transcendence, participating with its universe in eternity.

Thus a mythology is a control system, on the one hand framing its community to accord with an intuited order of nature and, on the other hand, by means of its symbolic pedagogic rites, conducting individuals through the ineluctable psychophysiological stages of transformation of a human lifetime—birth, childhood and adolescence, age, old age, and the release of death—in unbroken accord simultaneously with the requirements of this world and the rapture of participation in a manner of being beyond time. For all the symbolic narratives, images, rites, and festivals by which life within the cultural monad is controlled and defined are of the order of the way of art. Their effect, therefore, is to wake the intellect to realizations equivalent to those of the insights that produced them.

In a paper by Ananda K. Coomaraswamy, introduced by a quotation from Walt Whitman—"These things are really the thoughts of all men in all ages and lands, they are not original with me"—the point is made with respect to the metaphorical language of mythology and metaphysics that "its 'worlds' and 'gods' are levels of reference and symbolic entities which are neither places nor individuals but states of being realizable within you."[7]

A mythology is, in this sense, an organization of metaphorical figures connotative of states of mind that are not finally of this or that place and time, notwithstanding that the figures themselves initially suggest such localization. My magnificent master and great friend of many years ago, Heinrich Zimmer (1890–1943), had a saying: "The best things can't be told: the second best are misunderstood." The second best are misunderstood because, as metaphors poetically of that which cannot be told, they are misread prosaically as referring to tangible facts. The connoted messages are thus lost in the symbols, the elementary ideas in local "ethnic" inflections.

Inevitably, in the popular mind, where such metaphors of transcendence become known only as represented in the rituals and legends of the local, mythologically inspired control system, the whole sense of the symbology remains locked to local practical aims and ethical ideals, in the function chiefly of controlling, socializing, and harmonizing in strictly local terms the primitive bioenergies of the human animal, to the popular ends of health, progeny, and prosperity as the proper aims of a human life. Whereas, in fundamental contrast, the way of the mystic and of proper art (and we might also add, religion) is of recognizing *through* the metaphors an epiphany beyond words. For, as told in the Kena Upaniṣad: "There the eye goes not, speech goes not, nor the mind. We know not, nor can we imagine, how to convey it. For it is other than the known; also, beyond the unknown. Thus we have heard from the ancients, who have told of it.... *If known here, then there is truth; if not known, there is great destruction.* The wise, discerning it in *all* beings, become on departing this world, immortal."[8]

For some reason which I have not yet found anywhere explained, the popular, unenlightened practice of prosaic reification of metaphoric imagery has been the fundamental method of the most influential exegetes of the whole Judeo-Christian-Islamic mythic complex. The idea of the Virgin Birth, for example, is argued as a historical fact, whereas in practically every mythology of the world instances have appeared of this elementary idea. American Indian mythologies abound in virgin births. Therefore, the intended reference of the archetypal image cannot possibly have been to a supposed occurrence in the Near East in the first century B.C. The elementary idea, likewise, of the Promised Land cannot originally have referred to a part of this earth to be conquered by military might, but to a place of spiritual peace in the heart, to be discovered through contemplation. Creation myths, furthermore, which, when read in their mystical sense might bring to mind the idea of a background beyond time out of which the whole temporal world with its colorful populations has been derived, when read, instead, historically, only justify as supernaturally endowed the moral order of some local culture. In short, the social, as opposed to the mystical function of a mythology, is not to open the mind, but to enclose it: to bind a local people together in mutual support by offering images that awaken the heart to recognitions of commonality, without allowing these to escape the monadic compound.

It is surely evident, therefore, that whatever the future mythology of our soon-to-be-unified planet may be, its story of creation and the evolution of civilizations shall not be turned to the magnification of any one, two, or three of the innumerable monadic instances in the vast polymorphic display.

Our scientists and historians have already laid out the plot. And the way in which the monads there appear and melt away in the vision of a single mighty presence playing hide-and-seek with itself on the ever-turning stage of what James Joyce in *Finnegans Wake* has called "The Hereweareagain Gaieties"9 is a rapture to behold. For as the various ethnic forms dissolve, it is the image of androgynous Anthropos that emerges through and among them. "Surely," as the poet Yeats perceived, "some revelation is at hand."

Meanwhile, however, in the old Near East, where in Sargon's time the idea appears to have first been implemented of politically exploitive wars of territorial conquest, contending armies of the only three monotheistic monads of the planet (each dedicated to a notion of its own historically conditioned idea of "God" as having been from all eternity, in very fact, that to which, not words, nor the eye, nor the mind can reach) in this delicate moment of imminent global unification, "Year of Our Lord" (A.D.) 1985, are threatening the whole process of global unification with the adventure of their scripturally prophesied Armageddon.

> Surely some revelation is at hand.
> Surely the Second Coming is at hand.
> The Second Coming! Hardly are those words out
> When a vast image out of Spiritus Mundi
> Troubles my sight; somewhere in sands of the desert
> A shape with lion body and the head of a man,
> A gaze blank and pitiless as the sun,
> Is moving its slow thighs, while all about it
> Reel shadows of the indignant desert birds.
> The darkness drops again; but now I know
> That twenty centuries of stony sleep
> Were vexed to nightmare by a rocking cradle,
> And what rough beast, its hour come round at last,
> Slouches towards Bethlehem to be born?10

CHAPTER I

COSMOLOGY AND THE
MYTHIC IMAGINATION

It was a startling experience for me, as it must have been for many others watching the television broadcast of the Apollo spaceflight immediately before that of Armstrong's landing on the moon, when Ground Control in Houston asked, "Who's navigating now?" and the answer that came back was, "Newton!"

I was reminded of Immanuel Kant's discussion of space in his *Prolegomena to Any Future Metaphysics,* where he asks: "How is it that in this space, here, we can make judgments that we know with apodictic certainty will be valid in that space, there?"[1]

The little module was out beyond the moon. That was a part of space that no one had ever before visited. Yet the scientists in Houston knew exactly how much energy to eject from those jets, when turned in just what direction, to bring the module down from outer space to within a mile of a battleship waiting for it in the Pacific Ocean.

Kant's reply to the question was that the laws of space are known to the mind because they are *of* the mind. They are of a knowledge that is within us from birth, a knowledge *a priori,* which is only brought to recollection by apparently external circumstance. During the following flight, when Armstrong's booted foot came down to leave its imprint on the surface of the moon, no one knew how deeply it might sink into lunar dust. That was to be knowledge *a posteriori,* knowledge from experience, knowledge *after* the event. But how to bring the module down, and how to get it up there, had been known from the beginning. Moreover, those later spacecraft that are now cruising far out beyond the moon, in what is known as outer space! It is known exactly how to maneuver them, to bring messages back, to turn them around, even to correct their faults.

In other words, it then occurred to me that outer space is within inasmuch as the laws of space are within us; outer and inner space are the same. We know, furthermore, that we have actually been born from space, since it was out of primordial space that the galaxy took form, of which our life-giving sun is a member. And this earth, of whose material we are made, is a flying satellite of that sun. We are, in fact, productions of this earth. We are, as it were, its organs. Our eyes are the eyes of this earth; our knowledge is the earth's knowledge. And the earth, as we now know, is a production of space.

Alerted by such remotely intimate thoughts, and deciding to learn something more *(a posteriori)* about the anatomy of our great-grandmother, Space, I turned for information to that remarkable world atlas (actually, an atlas of the universe), which had been issued as the fifth edition (1981) of the *National Geographic Atlas of the World.* I had thought myself already somewhat informed of the findings of those scientists who man the great telescopes on our mountaintops (the eyes and ears of our planet); but what I learned from the first fifteen pages of that volume amazed me. There is one two-page spread on which our solar system is pictured, and then the galaxy of billions of stars within which this solar system rides, and then the cluster of twenty galaxies of which our galaxy is a member, which local cluster, in turn, is represented as but one of thousands of such local clusters of galaxies, themselves gathered in superclusters in a universe whose limits are not yet known.

What those pages opened to me, in short, was the vision of a universe of unimaginable magnitude and inconceivable violence: billions upon billions—literally!—of roaring thermonuclear furnaces scattering from each other, each thermonuclear furnace being a star, and our sun among them: many of them actually blowing themselves to pieces, littering the outermost reaches of space with dust and gas, out of which new stars with circling planets are being born right now. And then, from still more remote distances, beyond all these, there come murmurs—microwaves— which are echoes of the greatest cataclysmic explosion of all, namely the Big Bang of creation, which, according to recent reckonings, must have occurred some 18 billion years ago.

The Big Bang of creation! Out of what did it arise?

The account resembles, in a way, that of the first verses of the Latin poet Ovid's *Metamorphoses* (composed in the first decade A.D.*),* where he writes that originally there was a formless chaos of miscellaneous elements, dis-arranged, vaguely floating; and that *deus,* a "god," brought order out of this chaos, sending the elements—fire, air, water, and earth—to their places.

From the atlas (and then some further reading) I learned that, origi-nally, what has been described both as a "great featureless mass" and (more mysteriously and, therefore, perhaps more accurately) as an "impulse" (Ovid's *deus)* reached a maximum of concentration that could be sustained no more than a billionth of a second when (and right here, the Big Bang) the inconceivable pressure of an entire incipient universe confined to a single point became converted into energy and mass, the primal twin man-ifestations of all perceived "reality" in what is known to the mind as space-time (Sanskrit, *māyā).* [2] A sphere of ravening intensity began spreading at the speed of light and, as "space" cooled, within the first second, muons and neutrinos had been followed by protons and neutrons, with nuclei cap-turing electrons and atoms coming into existence. The degree of heat was indescribable. It has been cooling ever since, while the whole event con-tinues to expand with its initial velocity.

And so we come to the picture of this universe today, as disclosed by those marvelous instruments put to use by our astronomers, which are de-livering to them a revelation of millions of spinning galaxies, many as great as our Milky Way and each with billions of stars, all moving at prodigious rates away from one another, and *with no still point* anywhere. An epochal series of experiments conducted in Ohio in the middle 1880s (published 1887) by two American scientists, A. A. Michelson and Edward W. Morley (the Michelson-Morley experiment), which had demonstrated definitively that the classic notion could no longer be entertained of a universal ether against which interstellar velocities might be comparatively measured, resulted in 1905 in Albert Einstein's founding statement of the modern theory of relativity: "It is impossible by any experiment whatsoever to determine absolute rest." Any place you like may be chosen for your hypothetical still point, and from any such tentative, operational center, what you would see would be this streaming away of those myriads of galaxies going into distance, the furthest of them at such distances that, finally, our greatest telescopes lose track of them entirely—the light coming from them arriving so late that their present positions are out of sight.

And so now, of all the possible centers, our own earth, of course, is the only one available to us. Revolving on its own axis once every twenty-four hours, this operational still point is annually circling one of the several hundred billion suns that constitute our galaxy, this sun itself meanwhile traveling at the rate of 136 miles per second around the periphery of our native galaxy, circling it once every 230 million years. The diameter of this galaxy, this Milky Way of exploding stars, is now described as 100,000 light years, a light year being the distance light travels in one year. But light travels at the rate of 186,000 miles per second, and the number of seconds in a year (if I calculate correctly) is 31,557,600. So that if we multiply 186,000 miles by 31,557,600 seconds, we arrive at the idea of one light year, which is, namely (if again I calculate correctly), 5 trillion, 869 billion, 713 million, 600 thousand miles. And 100,000 of these will then amount to 586 quadrillion, 971 trillion, 360 billion (586,971,360,000,000,000) miles. And within this galaxy of that diameter, the nearest sun to our sun, nearest star to our star, is Alpha in Centauri, which is about 4 light years, which is to say, a mere 25 trillion miles, away.

From our position in this inconceivable galaxy, when we look up at night at the Milky Way, we are sighting, as it were, along the radius of a great disk. The other stars that we see in the night sky are members also of this galaxy, but are situated to one side or the other of the crosscut. And this disk, this galaxy of which our sun is a minor member, is but one of what is known to science as a "local group" of galaxies, the number in our particular group being twenty: twenty Milky Ways of billions of exploding nuclear furnaces, flying from each other through spaces not to be measured, the universe (of which we speak so easily) comprising, literally, quintillions of such self-consuming stars.

And so now we must ask: What does all this do to mythology? Obviously, some corrections have to be made.

For example: It is believed that Jesus, having risen from the dead, ascended physically to heaven (Luke 24:51), to be followed shortly by his mother in her sleep (Early Christian belief, confirmed as Roman Catholic dogma on November 1, 1950). It is also written that some nine centuries earlier, Elijah, riding a chariot of fire, had been carried to heaven in a whirlwind (2 Kings 2:11).

Now, even ascending at the speed of light, which for a physical body is impossible, those three celestial voyagers would not yet be out of the galaxy. Dante in the year A.D. 1300 spent the Easter weekend in a visit to hell, purgatory, and heaven; but that voyage was in spirit alone, his body remaining on earth. Whereas Jesus, Mary, and Elijah are declared to have ascended physically. What is to be made today of such mythological (hence, metaphorical) folk ideas?

Obviously, if anything of value is to be made of them at all (and I submit that the elementary original idea must have been something of this kind), where those bodies went was not into outer space, but into inner space. That is to say, what is connoted by such metaphorical voyages is the possibility of a return of the mind in spirit, while still incarnate, to full knowledge of that transcendent source out of which the mystery of a given life arises into this field of time and back into which it in time dissolves. It is an old, old story in mythology: of the Alpha and Omega that is the ground of all being, to be realized as the beginning and end of this life. The imagery is necessarily physical and thus apparently of outer space. The inherent connotation is always, however, psychological and metaphysical, which is to say, of inner space. When read as denoting merely specified events, therefore, the mirrored inward images lose their inherent spiritual force and, becoming overloaded with sentiment, only bind the will the more to temporality.

There is a beautiful saying of Novalis: "The seat of the soul is there, where the outer and the inner worlds meet." That is the wonderland of myth. From the outer world the senses carry images to the mind, which do not become myth, however, until there transformed by fusion with accordant insights, awakened as imagination from the inner world of the body. The Buddhists speak of Buddha Realms. These are planes and orders of consciousness that can be brought to mind through meditations on appropriately mythologized forms. Plato tells of universal ideas, the memory of which is lost at birth but through philosophy may be recalled.[3] These correspond to Bastian's "elementary ideas" and Jung's "archetypes of the collective unconscious." In India, as noticed by Ananda K. Coomarasway,[4] works of art representing indifferent objects, local personages and scenes, such as fill the walls and rooms of most of our museums, have been characterized as *deśī* ("local, popular, provincial") or as *nāgara* ("fashionable, worldly") and are regarded as esthetically insignificant; whereas those representing deities or revered ancestors, such as might appear in temples or on domestic shrines, are perceived as tokens of an inward, spiritual "way" or "path," termed *mārga,* which is a word derived from the vocabulary of the hunt, denoting the tracks or trail of an animal, by following which the hunter comes to his quarry. Similarly, the images of deities, which are but local forms of "elementary ideas," are footprints left, as it were, by local passages of the "Universal Self" *(ātman),* through contemplating which the worshiper attains "Self-Rapture" *(ātmānananda).* A passage from Plotinus may be quoted to this point: "Not all who perceive with eyes the sensible products of art are affected alike by the same object, but if they know it for the outward portrayal of an archetype subsisting in intuition, their hearts are shaken and they recapture memory of that Original."[5]

All mythologies, finally, are works of art of this order and effect. Sociologically and psychologically, however, it makes a great difference what images they present; for the degree of their opening of inner space is a function of the reach into outer space that they unclose. In the earliest, most limited and limiting mythologies of which we have knowledge, for example, the horizons are local and tribal. Such mythologies are neither addressed to, nor concerned with, humanity at large. The tribe and its landscape are the universe. Read again the first, second, third, and fourth chapters of the Book of Genesis. Such a tiny, minute affair! What relation does such a cosmology bear to the universe now perceived? Or to the histories of any but one of the people of this earth? As stated unequivocally in 2 Kings 5:15, "There is no God in all the earth but in Israel." For at that time the center of the universe was Jerusalem. And the center of Jerusalem was the Temple. And the center of the Temple was the Holy of Holies in the Temple. And the center of the Holy of Holies was the Ark of the

Covenant therein. And the foundation of the universe was the Stone that was there before the Ark. Mythologically, metaphorically, that was a perfectly good cultic image. But it had nothing to do with the universe, or with the rest of the peoples of this planet.

Then came the year A.D. 70, the catastrophic destruction by the Romans of both Jerusalem and its temple and, following that, the historic dispersion of God's people among the Gentiles, the so-called Diaspora (Hebrew, *galut,* the "exile"), which threatened the very subsistence of what had been called in Ezra's time, the "holy race" (Ezra 9:12). Two subsequent centuries of rabbinical consultation, dialogue, and debate, however, as registered in the Mishna (that third century compilation of authoritative post-biblical laws, judgments, and determinations) sufficed to rescue the tradition by an adroit redefinition. The center now was to be known, not as a place, but as a people; not the Temple or the Ark, which meanwhile had disappeared, but the Israelite community over the earth. And so again in strictly ethnocentric terms, a tribal concept of the universe, its history, and its destiny (now highly intentional and sophisticated) was devised, having as its central feature the one and only holy thing upon all this earth: these people, themselves, of God's holy race.

In aboriginal societies, the tribal myths, while unexceptionally ethnocentric, do not anywhere exhibit such an exclusive fascination with the people themselves; for every feature of the landscape, the whole world of nature and everything around them, is encompassed in their regard. The earth for them is not of dust (Genesis 3:19), but alive and a mother. The animals and plants, and all the peoples dwelling on her bosom, are her children, also regarded in a sacred way. Moreover, the laws by which the people live, though from their ancestors and proper to themselves, do not elevate them beyond nature; nor are the gods and habits of their neighbors viewed as abominations (Ezra 9:1 and passim). Local cult and custom are recognized for what they are—namely, relative, not absolute—so that, although indeed limited and limiting, they may open the mind and heart to the world. For example:

There is an important little volume by the Nebraskan poet John Neihardt, *Black Elk Speaks,* in which the prophetic boyhood vision is recounted of an old Sioux medicine man, Keeper of the Sacred Pipe of his people, who at one point declared that in imagination he had seen himself standing on the central mountain of the world, which in his view, of course, was nowhere near Jerusalem, but Harney Peak, in the Black Hills of South Dakota. And while there, "I was seeing in a sacred manner," he said, "the shapes of all things in the spirit, and the shape of all things as they must live together, like one being. And I saw that the sacred hoop of my people was one of many hoops that made one circle, wide as daylight and as starlight, and in the center grew one mighty flowering tree to shelter all the children of one mother and one father."[6]

Thus from the humanity of an awakened inner eye and consciousness, a vision released from the limitations of its local, tribal horizon might open to the world and even to transcendence. For, as Black Elk remarked to Neihardt when telling of this vision beheld from Harney Peak, South Dakota, as center of the world: "But anywhere is the center of the world."[7]

There, I would say, was a *true* prophet, who knew the difference between his ethnic ideas and the elementary ideas that they enclose, between a metaphor and its connotation, between a tribal myth and its metaphysical import. For when the inner eye is awakened and a revelation arises from inner space to meet impressions brought by the senses from outer space to the mind, the significance of the conjunction is lost unless the outward image opens to receive and embody the elementary idea—this being the whole sense of the transformation of nature in art. Otherwise, nothing has happened; an external event has been merely documented and a cultic, ethnic centricity given as the last word of religion, with naturalism the end and beginning of art.

A decisive, enormous leap out of the confines of all local histories and landscapes occurred in Mesopotamia in the fourth millennium B.C., during the period of the rise of the ziggurats, those storied temple towers, symbolic of the *axis mundi,* which are caricatured in the Bible as the Tower of Babel. The leap was from geography to the cosmos, beyond the moon, whereupon the primal, limited, and limiting tribal manner of thought (which the Hebrew prophets chose deliberately to retain) was by the Gentile civilizations left behind. That was the period when writing was invented; also, mathematical measurement, and the wheel. The priestly watchers of the night skies at that time were the first in the world to recognize that there is a mathematical regularity in the celestial passages of the seven visible spheres—the sun, the moon, Mercury, Venus, Mars, Jupiter, and Saturn—along the heaven-way of the Zodiac. And with that, the idea dawned of a cosmic order, *mathematically* discoverable, which it should be the function of a governing priesthood to translate from its heavenly revelation into an order of civilized human life. The idea of the hieratic city-state made its appearance at that time, with kings and queens symbolically attired, enacting together with their courts an aristocratic mime in imitation of the celestial display, the king crowned as the moon or sun, his queen and the other members of their court as planetary presences. And those allegorical identifications were taken seriously to such a degree that when celestial signs appeared that were interpreted as marking the end of an eon, the kings and queens, together with their courts, were ceremoniously buried alive. Sir James G. Frazer, in *The Golden Bough* (12 volumes, 1907–1915), published evidence from many parts of the world of the practice of such rites. Buried courts have been unearthed from Sumer and Egypt to China.

Some notion of the whole profoundly conceived, macro-microcosmic import of such courtly mimes may be gained from a consideration of the mathematics of the mythological and actual cycles of the calendars to which such rites were attached. For example, in the Hindu sacred epics and Purāṇas (popular tellings of ancient lore), the number of years reckoned to the present cycle of time, the so-called Kālī Yuga, is 432,000; the number reckoned to the "great cycle" *(mahāyuga)* within which this *yuga* falls being 4,320,000. But then reading one day in the Icelandic Eddas, I discovered that in Othin's (Wotan's) warrior hall, Valhöll, there were 540 doors, through each of which, on the "Day of the Wolf" (that is to say, at the end of the present cycle of time), there would pass 800 divine warriors to engage the antigods in a battle of mutual annihilation.[8] 800 x 540 = 432,000. And so I asked myself how it might ever have come to pass that in tenth-to-thirteenth century Iceland the same number of years were reckoned to the present cycle of time as in India.

In Babylon, I then recalled, there had been a Chaldean priest, Berossos, who, c. 280 B.C., had rendered into Greek an account of the history and mythology of Babylonia, wherein it was told that between the time of the rise of the first city, Kish, and the coming of the Babylonian mythological flood (from which that of the Bible is taken), there elapsed 432,000 years, during which antediluvian era, ten kings reigned. Very long lives! Longer even than Methuselah's (Genesis 5:27), which had been of only 969.

So I turned to the Old Testament (Genesis 5) and counting the number of antediluvian patriarchs, Adam to Noah, discovered, of course, that they were ten. How many years? Adam was 130 years old when he begat Seth, who was 105 when he begat Enosh, and so on, to Noah, who was 600 years old when the flood came: to a grand total, from the first day of Adam's creation to the first drop of rain of Noah's flood, of 1,656 years. Any relation to 432,000? Julius Oppert, a distinguished Jewish Assyriologist of the last century, in 1877 presented before the Royal Society for Sciences in Göttingen a paper on "Dates in Genesis,"[9] in which it was shown that in 1,656 years there are 86,400 seven-day weeks. 86,400 ÷ 2 = 43,200.

Antediluvian Patriarch	Age When Begetting Son	Age at Time of Death
1. Adam (Genesis 5:3–5)	130	930
2. Seth (ib. 5:6–8)	105	912
3. Enosh (ib. 5:9–11)	90	905
4. Kenon (ib. 5:12–14)	70	910
5. Mahalalel (ib. 5:15–17)	65	895
6. Jared (ib. 5:18–20)	162	962
7. Enoch (ib. 5:21–24)	65	365
8. Methuselah (ib. 5:25–27)	187	969
9. Lamech (ib. 5:28–31)	182	767
10. Noah (ib. 7:6), who was	600 years old when the Flood came.	
Grand Total from Creation:	1,656 years to year of the Flood.	

And so it appears that in the Book of Genesis there are two contrary theologies represented in relation to the legend of the Deluge. One is the old tribal, popular tale of a willful, personal creator-god, who saw that "the wickedness of man was great in the earth . . . and was sorry that he had made man on the earth, and it grieved him to his heart. So the Lord said, 'I will blot out man whom I have created from the face of the ground, man and beast and creeping things and birds of the air, for I am sorry that I have made them'" (Genesis 6:5–7). The other idea, which is in fundamental contrast, is that of the disguised number, 86,400, which is a deeply hidden reference to the Gentile, Sumero-Babylonian, *mathematical* cosmology of the ever-revolving cycles of impersonal time, with whole universes and their populations coming into being, flowering for a season of 43,200 (432,000 or 4,320,000) years, dissolving back into the cosmic mother-sea to rest for an equal spell of years before returning, and so again, again, and again. The Jews, it will be remembered, were for fifty years exiled from their capital to Babylon (586–539 B.C.), when they were subject, willy nilly, to Babylonian influences, so that although the popular, exoteric version of their Deluge legend is from the period of David's kingdom, tenth century or so B.C., the exquisitely secreted indication of a priestly knowledge, beyond that, of a larger, cyclic version of the legend—where the god himself would have come into being and gone out of being with the universe of which he was the lord—is post-Exilic, as are, also, the genealogical datings of Genesis chapter 5, which are so very nicely contrived to join the 600 years of Noah's age at the time of the Flood to furnish a total exactly of 1,656.

It is to be noticed, by the way, that $1 + 6 + 5 + 6 = 18$, which is twice 9, while $4 + 3 + 2 = 9$: 9 being a number traditionally associated with the Goddess Mother of the World and its gods. In India the number of recited names in a litany of this goddess is 108. $1 + 0 + 8 = 9$, while $108 \times 4 = 432$. In Roman Catholic Europe, when the Angelus tolls (at morning, noon, and evening), it rings $3 + 3 + 3$ and then 9 times, in celebration of the Virgin's conception of the Savior. The recited prayer at those junctures, "The angel of the Lord declared unto Mary, and she conceived by the Holy Ghost.... and THE WORD WAS MADE FLESH... " is in recognition of this miracle at the opening of a new world age. In ancient Greece, 9 was the number of the Muses, patron goddesses of the arts. They were the daughters of Mnemosyne ("memory"), the source of imagination, which in turn is the carrier of archetypal, elementary ideas to artistic realization in the field of space-time. The number 9, that is to say, relates traditionally to the Great Goddess of Many Names (Devī, Inanna, Ishtar, Astarte, Artemis, Venus, etc.), as matrix of the cosmic process, whether in the macrocosm or in a microcosmic field of manifestation. The reason for the suppression of her image by a clergy interested in the claims only of a divinity heavily bearded, therefore, can be readily surmised; but why the same company of priestly doctors so artfully concealed in their document an unmistakable notice of their own knowledge of her power awaits interpretation.

The profundity and sublime majesty of the suppressed mythology can be appreciated best by way of two apparently unrelated clocks, one, the ultimate clock of outer space, and the other of inner space—respectively, the astronomical precession of the equinoxes and the physiological beat of the human heart. Regarding the first: the slow westward motion, in the course of years, of the equinoctial points around the beltway of the zodiac (the vernal equinox, for example, moving from the sign of Aries, where it had been before the birth of Christ, through Pisces, where it is now, toward Aquarius, where it will be in a couple of hundred years), requires for one complete cycle of the twelve zodiacal signs exactly 25,920 years, which term is known as a "great" or "Platonic" year. But if we divide 25,920 by 60 (which is the ancient Mesopotamian *soss,* or basic sexagesimal unit of astronomical measurement, still used in the measurement of circles, whether of time or of space), the quotient is 432. Moreover: 2 + 5 + 9 + 2 + 0 = 18.

And regarding the second, the inward clock: I have read in a popular book on physical education that "A conditioned man, who exercises regularly, will have a resting heart rate of about 60 beats per minute or less.... Sixty per minute times 60 minutes, equals 3,600 beats per hour. Times 24 hours, equals 86,400 beats a day."[10]

It is strange that in our history books the discovery of the precession of the equinoxes should be attributed always to the Greek Hipparchus, second century B.C., when the magic number 432 (which when multiplied by 60 produces 25,920) was already employed in the reckoning of major cycles of time before that century. How long before, we do not know. But the Chaldean priest Berossos was of the early third century B.C., and the mythology of which he wrote the account was allegedly of Babylon before its conquest by the Persians in 539 B.C. Babylonian mythology, furthermore, was a late development out of the very much earlier Sumerian of c. 3000–2000 B.C.; and our earliest known legend of the universal flood is from Sumer. To suggest that already in the ziggurats of Sumer the priests were reckoning in terms of the precession of the equinoxes would be perhaps too bold. There is every reason to believe, however, that the mythology into which, at some unknown date, the astonishingly accurate numerical insight was introduced had been Sumerian, indeed even possibly pre-Sumerian; for by the end of the third millennium B.C. it was already known to all the civilizations at that time in flower from the Nile valley and Aegean Sea to the Indus.

The mystery of the night sky, those enigmatic passages of slowly but steadily moving lights among the fixed stars, had delivered the revelation, when charted mathematically, of a cosmic order, and in response, from the depths of the human imagination, a reciprocal recognition had been evoked. A vast concept took form of the universe as a living being in the likeness of a great mother, within whose womb all the worlds, both of life and of death, had their existence (see Figure 1). And the human body is in miniature a duplicate of that macrocosmic form. So that throughout the whole an occult harmony prevails, which it is the function of a mythology and relevant rites to make known. The Chinese idea of the *tao* is a development out of this macro-microcosmic insight. Hinduism in all its aspects carries into every act of life the idea of *dharma* ("virtue") as conformity to the caste laws of one's birth, which are understood to be, not of social invention, but given of nature, like the laws of action of the various animal species. The noun *dharma* is from a verbal root *dhri* ("to hold, to bear, to support"). For by conforming perfectly to one's *dharma (sva-dharma)*, as do the various animal species to theirs, the plants to theirs, and the sun, the moon, the planets, and the stars to theirs, one at once supports the universe and is supported by it. And so, indeed, in our modern Western world, when a doctor takes a patient's pulse, if the beat is sixty a minute (43,200 in twelve hours), it is the pulse of a conditioned athlete in accord at once with his own nature and with the rhythm of the universe: the function of medicine, like that of mythology and ritual, being to keep mankind in accord with the natural order.*

Well and good enough, one might suppose! However—and here is where the West begins—a radical and enormously influential ethical protest against the uncritical submission to the will in nature that is implicit in this finally *mystical* world vision broke forth in Iran, some time in

---

* A startling microcosmic revelation of the mystic force of this number came recently to light when engineers in the Wilson Sporting Goods laboratories testing (for distance) golf balls with anywhere from 30 to 1,212 dimples were advised by computer that the optimum number would be 432. For indeed, the Wilson 432 golf ball has been found by professionals to lengthen their drives some ten to thirteen or more yards.

the second or first millenium B.C., in the dualistic religious view of Zarathustra (known to the Greeks as Zoroaster). The dates of this earliest known prophet of an absolute distinction between good and evil—in contrast to the cosmological, mystical insight—are in dispute. Some scholars place him c. 1200 B.C.; others, six to seven centuries later. In either case, the god of light and truth and justice whose gospel he preached, Ahura Mazda, was the god professed by the Persian King of Kings, Darius I (ruled 521–486 B.C.), during whose reign the first moves were undertaken to return the Jews to Jerusalem; and that Zoroastrian patterns of thought and verbal stereotypes were absorbed into Pharasaic as well as into Essene Judaism, there is today no question. The recently discovered Essene Dead Sea Scroll known as "The War of the Sons of Light and the Sons of Darkness," for example, is a classic instance of Zoroastrian ethical dualism, fused, however, with the Jewish tribal notion of themselves as the one and only people of God. As the "Sons of Light," at the end of time, in a holy war of exactly thirty-five years with a year of rest every seventh, they are to attack and overcome in programmed stages, with timely help from the great hand of God, all the Gentile nations, the "Sons of Darkness," of this earth. [11]

Figure 1. Jaina world image in the form of a great goddess. Gouache on cloth, 15 x 11 inches. Rajasthan, eighteenth century.

At the level of the waist is the plane of earth. Below are the purgatories and above the heavens to which "souls" *(jīvas)* descend or ascend between incarnations, according to their lives. *Ahiṁsa*, "non-injury, or nonviolence," is for the Jains the determining virtue. The aim is to ascend, completely cleansed of impulse to "action," *(karma)*, to the gaining of "release" *(mokṣa)* from the "round of rebirths" *(saṁsāra)* in the removed realm here shown as above the brows of the cosmic being. This "release" is not conceived of in Jainism as it is in Hinduism and Buddhism, as a *nirvāṇa* of nonentity, but as *kaivalyam,* a state of unconditioned, isolated perfection in timeless omniscience.

Mahāvīra (c. 599–527 B.C.), last of the twenty-four founding "Conquerors" *(jinas),* or teachers of the way to this victory, was an older contemporary of the Buddha (c. 563–483 B.C.). The number of his named predecessors reaches back beyond historical time into ages purely mythological. There can be no doubt that already in the period of the Indus Civilization, c. 2300–1750 B.C., there were in India practitioners of an austere type of yoga who may indeed have been of the Jina line. See Figures 5 and 6 (page 46).

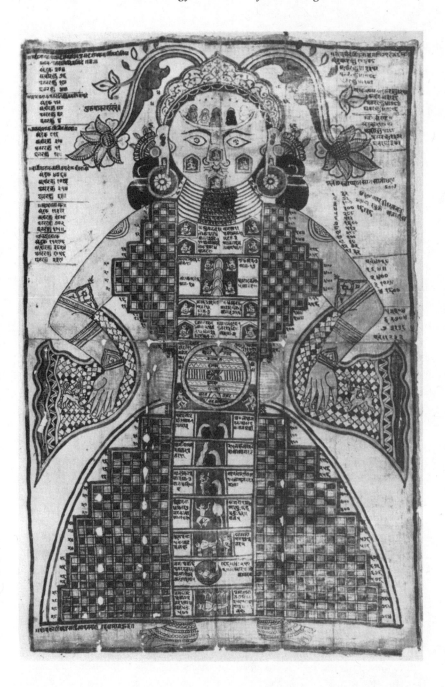

For according to Zarathustra, there were two creator-gods—a good god, Ahura Mazda, of light, of truth, and of justice, and an evil god, Angra Mainyu, of darkness, deception, and malice. In the beginning, Ahura Mazda created a universe of virtue and light, which Angra Mainyu then maliciously corrupted; so that the world in which we live is mixed of good and evil. Man is therefore not to put himself in accord with nature—as in the ancient and oriental worlds—but to make a decision for the good, put himself in accord with the good, fight for justice and the light, and correct nature.

The nature of the first man, Gayomart, was corrupted by the malice of Angra Mainyu. Man, therefore, is "fallen man." His nature is not to be trusted. A great prophet, however, Zarathustra, has come into the world, born, they say, of a virgin, who has taught the way of virtue which is to lead in the end to a restoration of Ahura Mazda's uncorrupted universe. In a prodigious final battle, the powers of light and justice, led by a radiant reincarnation, Saoshyant, of the seed of the prophet Zarathustra, born again a virgin, will engage, overwhelm, and destroy the whole production of Angra Mainyu, indeed even Angra Mainyu himself. The universe will be cleared of darkness, and the dead, now purged of death, will be resurrected as bodies radiant of uncorrupted being.

Thus a completely new mythology arose, and instead of the ancient Sumero-Babylonian contemplation of the disappearances and reappearances of planets as revelatory of an order of nature with which society was to be held in accord, an idea of good and evil, light and dark, even of life and death as separable took hold, and the prophecy was announced of a progressive restoration to righteousness of the order of nature. Where formerly there had been the planetary cycles, marking days and nights, the months, years, and eons of unending time, there was now to be a straight line of progressive world history with a beginning, a middle, and a prophesied end—Gayomart, Zarathustra, and Saoshyant: Adam, Jesus, and the Second Coming. Where formerly there had been, as the ideal, harmony with the whole, there was now discrimination, a decision to be made, "not peace, but a sword" (Matthew 10:34), effort, struggle, and zeal, in the name of a universal reform. In the Persian empire this ethical world-ideal became identified with the political aims of the King of Kings himself, who reigned as the regent of Ahura Mazda; in Christendom, by a sort of spiritual contagion, *Gott mit uns* has ever been the war cry of every national army, on both sides of the line; while throughout the territorial reaches of Islam, the rhetoric of righteousness has been epitomized in the matched phrases, *dar al'islām* ("the realm of submission [to Allah]") and *dar al'harb* ("the realm of war"), which is to say, the rest of the world.

And so throughout the complex of mythologies now operative in the West—which by virture of their common impulse to missionary imperialism are today reshaping the planet, save where the no less reformational zeal of the mission of Karl Marx has taken over the enterprise—the reaches of outer space to which the religious mind is formally directed are not cosmic, but geographical, and defined in terms, moreover, of dark and light, God's portion *(dar al'islām)* and the devil's *(dar al'harb);* prayers still being addressed in all seriousness to a named and defined masculine personality inhabiting a local piece of sky a short flight beyond the moon.

Meanwhile, certain spiritually significant changes have occurred in the psychophysical environment of our species. The first, of course, followed the publication, A.D. 1543, of Copernicus's "Six Books on the Revolutions of the Celestial Orbs" *(De revolutionibus orbium coelestium libri VI),* when the sun displaced the earth at the center of God's universe; so that, whereas our eyes see the sun rise daily in the east, hang high in the heavens at noon, and go down in glory in the west, what our brains now know is nothing of the kind. With that fateful publication, the recognized *idea* of the earth in relation to outer space became forever separated from the daily *experience* of the same. An intellectual *concept* had refuted and displaced the nevertheless persistent sensory *percept.* The heliocentric universe has never been translated into a mythology. Science and religion have therewith gone apart. And that is the case to the present hour, with the problem even compounded by our present recognition of the inconceivable magnitude of this galaxy of stars, of which our life-giving sun is a peripheral member, circling with its satellites in this single galaxy among millions within a space of incredible distances, having no fixed form or end.

"Have you not heard," asked Nietzsche, already in the introduction to his *Thus Spake Zarathustra* (1883–84): "Have you not yet heard that God is dead?"—the god in point, of course, being the named and defined creator-god of the historically limited Bible. For the conditions, not only of life, but of thought also, have considerably changed since the centuries of the composition of that guide to truth and virtue, which with its deliberately restricted and restricting ethnocentric horizon and tribal "jealous God" (Exodus 20:5) is culture specific to such a degree that its "folk ideas" and "elementary ideas" are inseparably fused.

The first step to mystical realization is the leaving of such a defined god for an experience of transcendence, disengaging the ethnic from the elementary idea, *for any god who is not transparent to transcendence is an idol, and its worship is idolatry.* Also, the first step to participation in the destiny of humanity today, which is neither of this folk nor of that, but of the whole population of this globe, is to recognize every such local image of a god as but one of many thousands, millions, even perhaps billions, of locally useful symbolizations of that same mystery beyond sight or thought which our teachers have taught us to seek in their god alone. Black Elk's phrase, "The center is everywhere," is matched by a statement from a hermetic, early medieval text, *The Book of the Twenty-four Philosophers (Liber XXIV philosophorum):* "God is an infinite sphere, whose center is everywhere and circumference nowhere."[12] The idea, it seems to me, is in a most appropriate way illustrated in that stunning photograph (Figure 2) taken from the moon, and now frequently reproduced, of an earthrise, the earth rising as a radiant celestial orb, strewing light over a lunar landscape. Is the center the earth? Is the center the moon? The center is anywhere you like. Moreover, in that photograph from its own satellite, the rising earth shows none of those divisive territorial lines that on our maps are so conspicuous and important. The chosen center may be anywhere. The Holy Land is no special place. It is every place that has ever been recognized and mythologized by any people as home.

Moreover, this understanding of the ubiquity of the metaphysical center perfectly matches the lesson of the galaxies and of the Michelson-Morley finding that was epitomized in Einstein's representation of the utter impossibility of establishing absolute rest. It is the essence of relativity. And, when translated from the heavens to this earth, it implies that moral judgments depend likewise upon the relation of the frame of reference to the person or act being measured. "Judge not that you be not judged" (Matthew 7:1). There is no absolute good or evil. So that, as Nietzsche has suggested, if Zarathustra were to return today, his message would not be of good and evil as absolutes. The lesson of his first teaching, which was of integrity, has been learned. The lesson now, beyond good and evil, is to be of life. For as Nietzsche himself stated: "All ideals are dangerous, since they denigrate and stigmatize what is actual. They are poisons, which, however, as occasional medicaments, are indispensable."[13]

Figure 2. Earthrise over moon landscape. Photographed 1968, Apollo 8 Mission.

And so, in mythological terms, what is to happen now? All of our old gods are dead, and the new have not yet been born.

There is a medieval Hindu story in one of the Purāṇas, the Brahmavaivarta Purāṇa, of about the fifth century A.D., which concerns the

Vedic-Aryan tribal deity Indra, who is a mythological counterpart in India of Yahweh in the Near East, also of Olympian Zeus of the ancient Greeks, Ashur of the Assyrians, Tarhun of the Hittites, and so forth.

Those were all guardian family gods of the various nomadic herding tribes that throughout the second millennium B.C. were invading and assuming control of the cultivated lands and their temple-cities, all the way from southeastern Europe, across Asia Minor and the Near East, to the Indus Valley.

The chief gods of the invaders were predominantly male warrior gods, champions, each, of his special people. Those of the invaded agricultural territories, in contrast, were chiefly of the earth's fertility and life, local forms, for the most part, of the one great "Goddess of Many Names" (as she was later termed), of whom all beings, even gods and demons, are the progeny. Divinities of her kind are the local representatives of those powers of nature that indeed are the creative energies of all life. They are not of this day or that, but forever. Mythologies of the ever-returning cycles of unending time are everywhere of her order of being. So, too, are the mystical philosophies and meditational disciplines of the inward, individual quest for identification with the ground of one's own and the world's existence. In fundamental contrast, the sociological tribal gods are of a secondary, local-historical definition and relevance. They are of this people or that, this moment or that in the vast history of the universe. Moreover, their dwelling is not, and can never be, inward of nature, in the way of an immanent, pantheistic presence domiciled in the heart as the actuality of its life. As guardians, they are always invoked from "out there." They are lawgivers, support-givers to those they favor and to those alone, since they are not of nature, but of a people. Consequently, when such a secondary deity, on achieving at some historical moment mastery over a certain parcel of this earth, exalts himself to a posture of omnipotence, like the Aryan Indra in the following exemplary tale, the moment is at hand for a higher revelation.

There had been a period of drought and disaster over all the earth (or so it had seemed). A prodigious dragon, known as Vṛtra (the "Encloser") had for a thousand years enveloped and held within itself all the waters of the world's life. Planted fields lay waste. Cities were cities of the dead. Even the capital city of the gods, on the summit of Mount Sumeru, the pivotal center of the world, was in ruins. Then the vanquisher of demons, Indra, who is above all the Vedic-Aryan gods supreme, flung into the midst of the monstrous coils a thunderbolt that shattered the demon entirely. The waters burst free and streamed in ribbons over the land, to circulate once again through the body of the world.

That had been a mighty victory. The gods, the saints and sages, learning of it, flocked from all directions, their hearts pulsing with joy, to celebrate their champion as in glory he proceeded to the summit of Mount Sumeru. And when, upon arriving, he beheld the devastation, he summoned Vishvakarman to his side, the architect and craftsman of the Vedic pantheon, commissioning him to reconstruct the city in such a way as would be worthy of such a world savior as himself—which in one year that miraculous builder accomplished. In the center of that godly residence, radiant with innumerable gems, marvelous with towers, gardens, lakes, and palaces, stood the royal dwelling of the god Indra himself, incomparable in the world, with which, however, he was not even then satisfied. He had additional ideas: more lakes and palaces over there; a different sort of garden here! His vision of glory ever enlarging, he brought Vishvakarman to the point of despair. There was no escape for the craftsman till released by his insatiate employer.

Sick at heart, therefore, Vishvakarman turned for protection secretly to Brahmā, the universal creator, who abides far beyond and above the historical sphere of Indra's temporal victories. Brahmā sits enthroned on the radiant lotus of a cosmic dream represented as growing from the navel of the slumbering divinity, Viṣṇu (Vishnu). Metaphorically, that is to say, the universe together with Brahmā, its creator, is the emanation of some superior god's imagination. Viṣṇu is represented couched upon a prodigious seven-headed cobra named Ananta, which means "endless." The serpent floats upon the cosmic Milky Ocean that is the mother of us all. Its boundless energy gives the impulse that provokes the world-dreamer's dream and appears in space-time as the universe, that radiant lotus on which, not only Brahmā, but any god may be envisioned enthroned. It is in Viṣṇu's dream personified as his *śakti*, the goddess Padmā or Padmāvatī (Sanskrit, *padmā*, "lotus"), *śakti* being a term signifying "power, energy," and specifically, the active energy of a deity, personified as his wife.[14]

So when Vishvakarman, in secret prayer, had delivered to Brahmā the burden of his plea, the lotus-enthroned divinity responded, "O Blessed One, you shall tomorrow be quit of your task!" and descending from his lotus-support, the god proceeded to Vaikuntha in the northern ocean, where Viṣṇu couches upon Ananta, while the divine craftsman, unburdened, returned in peace to his work.

And indeed, next morning there appeared at the great gate of Indra's palace, surrounded by a cluster of children infatuated by his beauty, Viṣṇu himself in the form of a ten-year-old, blue-black boy attired in a white dhoti, with a bright religious mark painted on his forehead, a parasol in one hand and a pilgrim staff in the other. "O Porter," he said to the porter at the gate, "hurry and let your Indra know that a Brahmin has come to see him." Which the porter promptly did. And when Indra then arrived to greet his guest and beheld that smiling, beautiful child, he gladly invited him in. And having welcomed him with an offering of honey and milk and fruits, he asked: "O Venerable Boy, pray tell me the purpose of your coming."

Whereupon that lovely child, with a voice as soft and deep as of a gently thundering cloud replied, "O King of Gods, I have heard of the wonderful city and palace that you are building, and have come to refer to you a few questions that are in my mind. How many more years do you expect to spend in this magnificent construction? What further engineering feats will be required of Vishvakarman? O Greatest of the Gods, no Indra before you has ever completed such a residence."

Full of the wine of his triumph, the god broke into a loud laugh. "Indras before me?" he said. "Tell me, Child, how many might those Indras or Vishvakarmans be whom you have seen, or of whom you may have heard?"

The brahmin boy laughed as well. "My child," he answered; and his words, though gentle, delightful as nectar to the ears, sent through Indra, slowly, a chill: "Kashyapa, your father, I knew, the Old Tortoise Man, Lord Progenitor of All Creatures; also, Marichī, your grandfather, a saint whose only wealth lay in his devotion; likewise, Brahmā, offspring of the world-navel of Viṣṇu; and Viṣṇu, too, I know, the Preserver of Brahmā.

"O King of Gods, I have beheld the dreadful dissolution of the universe, when everything, every atom, melts into an immense sea, empty of life. No one can say how many universes there may be, or how many cycles of ages in each universe there may ever have been; how many Brahmās, how many Viṣṇus, how many Śivas. O King of Gods, there are those in your service who hold that it might be possible to number the particles of sand on earth, or drops of rain that fall from the sky, but no one will ever number all the Indras.

"The life and kingship of an Indra last, according to the divine standard of measure, seven eons; and the period of twenty-eight Indras amounts to one day and night of Brahmā. Brahmā's length of life is 108 years, according to that standard [108 x 4 = 432]. My Child, not to speak of Indras, of those Brahmās there is no end. Brahmā follows Brahmā. One sinks, the next arises. Nor can anyone estimate the number of the universes, side by side, at any moment of time, each containing a Brahmā, a Viṣṇu and a Śiva. Like delicate boats they float upon the fathomless, pure waters of the body of Mahā-Viṣṇu. And like the pores of the body of that Great Viṣṇu, those universes are numberless, each harboring no end of gods such as yourself."

A procession of ants in military formation had made its appearance on the floor of the great hall during the discourse of that beautiful boy, and when he saw them he laughed, but then fell silent and withdrew deeply into himself. Indra's lips, palate, and throat had gone dry. "Young Brahmin, why do you laugh?" he asked. "And who are you, here in the guise of a boy? To me you seem to be the Ocean of Virtue, concealed in deluding mist."

The magnificent child resumed. "I laughed because of those ants. The reason is a mystery. Do not ask me to disclose it. The seed of woe, as well as the source of all wisdom, is hidden in this secret. Like an ax it strikes at the root of the tree of worldly vanity; yet to those groping in darkness it is a lamp. Seldom revealed even to saints, buried in the wisdom of the ages, it is the living breath of ascetics, versed in the Vedas, who have renounced and transcended their mortality. But fools deluded by pride and desire it destroys."

The boy sank into silence, smiling, and Indra, unable to move, his lips, palate, and throat parched, presently asked, humbly: "O Son of a Brahmin, who you are I do not know. You seem to be Wisdom Incarnate. Disclose to me this secret of the ages, this light that dispels the dark."

Requested thus to teach, Viṣṇu in the guise of a boy opened to the god a hidden wisdom rarely revealed even to yogis. "O Indra," said he, "those marching ants that we saw in long parade, passing file by file, innumerable: each formerly was an Indra. Like you, each by virtue of selfless deeds once rose to the rank of a king of gods, but then, full of pride, self-serving, returned through many births to the condition of an ant. That was an army of former Indras.

"Piety and selfless deeds elevate the inhabitants of this earth to exalted spiritual estates: the condition of a brahmin, a king, an Indra, to the heaven of a Brahmā, a Viṣṇu, or a Śiva. But then, self-serving acts reduce them to the realms beneath, of sorrow and pain, rebirths among birds and vermin, or out of the wombs of pigs and beasts of the wild, or among trees. Action is a function of character, which in turn is controlled by custom. This is the whole substance of the secret. This knowledge is the ferry across the ocean of hell to beatitude.

"For all the animate and inanimate objects in this world, O Indra, are transitory, like dream. The gods on high, the mute trees and stones, are but apparitions in the fantasy. Good and evil attaching to a person are as perishable as bubbles. In the cycles of time they alternate. The wise are attached to neither." ·

An old yogi had entered while the beautiful boy was speaking. His head was piled high with matted hair, he wore a black deerskin around his loins, on his forehead a white religious mark was painted, and on his chest was a curious circle of hair, intact at the circumference, but from the center many hairs were gone. Over his head he held a parasol of grass. And coming directly between the king and the boy, he sat down on the floor like a lump of stone.

Then the great and glorious Indra, recovering his character as king, bowed to his stern guest, paid obeisance, and having offered him refreshments, honey and milk and fruits, bade him welcome; whereupon the boy, doing him reverence, began to ask the very questions the king would have proposed.

"O Holy Man," he said, "from where do you come? What is your name? And what brings you to this place? Where is your present home? What is the meaning of the grass parasol over your head? And what is the portent of that circular hairtuft on your chest: why is it dense at the circumference, but at the center almost bare? Be kind enough, O Holy Man, to answer these, my questions. I am curious to hear."

Patiently the old saint smiled and slowly began his reply. "O Young Brahmin, Hairy is my name. I have come here to see Indra. Since I know that my life is to be short, I have decided to possess no house of my own, neither to marry, nor to labor. For the present, begging is my livelihood, and to protect myself from rain and sun, I hold this parasol over my head. But as to this circle of hair on my chest, it is to the children of this world a source of fear, yet productive also of wisdom. With the fall of an Indra, one hair drops out. That is why in the center all the hairs are gone. When the rest of the period allotted to the present Brahmā will have expired, I myself shall die. O Brahmin Boy, it follows I am short of days. Why therefore a house, a wife, or a son?

"When every blink of the eyes of Viṣṇu marks the passing of a Brahmā, it necessarily follows that everything is as insubstantial as a cloud taking shape and dissolving. I therefore devote myself exclusively to meditation on the eviternal lotus feet of Viṣṇu. Rest in transcendent Viṣṇu is more than redemption, since every joy, even heavenly bliss, is fragile as a dream and only interferes with concentration on the Supreme.

"Śiva, the peace-bestowing, highest spiritual guide, taught me this wisdom," said the old man as he vanished. The boy also disappeared. And the king, Indra, sat alone, bewildered and unstrung.[15]

CHAPTER II

METAPHOR AS MYTH AND AS RELIGION

THE PROBLEM

From the point of view of any orthodoxy, myth might be defined simply as "other people's religion," to which an equivalent definition of religion would be "misunderstood mythology," the misunderstanding consisting in the interpretation of mythic metaphors as references to hard fact: the Virgin Birth, for example, as a biological anomaly, or the Promised Land as a portion of the Near East to be claimed and settled by a people chosen of God, the term "God" here to be understood as denoting an actual, though invisible, masculine personality, who created the universe and is now resident in an invisible, though actual, heaven to which the "justified" will go when they die, there to be joined at the end of time by their resurrected bodies.

What, in the name of Reason or Truth, is a modern mind to make of such evident nonsense?

Like dreams, myths are productions of the human imagination. Their images, consequently—though derived from the material world and its supposed history—are, like dreams, revelations of the deepest hopes, desires and fears, potentialities and conflicts, of the human will—which in turn is moved by the energies of the organs of the body operating variously against each other and in concert. Every myth, that is to say, whether or not by intention, is psychologically symbolic. Its narratives and images are to be read, therefore, not literally, but as metaphors.

Mythologies are addressed, however, as dreams normally are not, to questions of the origins, both of the natural world and of the arts, laws, and customs of a local people, *physical* things being understood in this view as *meta*physically grounded in a dreamlike mythological realm beyond space and time, which, since it is physically invisible, can be known only to the mind. And as the insubstantial shapes of dream arise from the formative ground of the individual will, so do all the passing shapes of the physical world arise (according to this way of thought) from a universal, morpho-genetic ground that is made known to the mind through the figurations of myth.

These mythic figurations are the "ancestral forms," the insubstantial archetypes, of all that is beheld by the eye as physically substantial, mate-rial things being understood as ephemeral concretions out of the energies of these noumena. Traditional forms of tools, dwellings, and weapons have their justification in such everlasting models. Rituals are direct expositions of their life-sustaining patterns. Temples and the narratives of myth are hermetic fields within which those apparitions known as gods and god-desses, demons, angels, demigods, incarnations, and the like typify in the guise of charismatic personalities the locally recognized vortices of con-sciousness out of which all aspects of the local theater of life derive their being. The figurations of myth are expressive, therefore, as those of dream normally are not, of a range of universal—as distinguished from specifi-cally individual—concerns. In vision the mind may expand to that cosmic range, as in the raptures of shamans and mystics; for the energies shaping the natural world are the same as those that operate through the organs of the human body. However, as noticed in the Chhāndogya Upaniṣad: "Just as those who do not know the spot might pass, time and again, over a hid-den treasure of gold without discovering it, so do all the creatures of this world pass daily into that Brahmā-world [in deep sleep] without discover-ing it, distracted as they are by false ideas."[1]

The distinguishing first function of a properly read mythology is to re-lease the mind from its naive fixation upon such false ideas, which are of material things as things-in-themselves. Hence, the figurations of myth are metaphorical (as dreams normally are not) in *two* senses simultaneously, as bearing (1) *psychological,* but at the same time (2) *metaphysical* connotations. By way of this dual focus the psychologically significant features of any local social order, environment, or supposed history can become transformed through myth into transparencies revelatory of transcendence.

Immanuel Kant has supplied an astonishingly simple formula for the interpretation of such dual statements. It appears in his fundamental *Prolegomena zu einer jeden künftigen Metaphysik, die als Wissenschaft wird auftreten können,* paragraphs 57–58. What there is offered is a four-term analogy (*a* is to *b* as *c* is to *x*), pointing not to an imperfect resemblance of two things, but to a perfect resemblance of two *relationships* between quite dissimilar things (*"nicht etwa, eine unvollkommene Änlichkeit zweier Dinge, sondern eine vollkommene Ähnlichkeit zweier Verhältnisse zwischen ganz unähnlichen Dingen"*): not "*a* somewhat resembles *b,*" but "the relationship of *a* to *b* perfectly resembles that of *c* to *x,*" where *x* represents a quantity that is not only unknown but absolutely unknowable—which is to say, is metaphysical.

Kant demonstrates the formula in two examples:

(1) As the promotion of the happiness of the children (*a*) is related to the parents' love (*b*), so is the welfare of the human race (*c*) to that unknown in God (*x*) which we call God's love; and

(2) The causality of the highest cause (*x*) is precisely, in respect to the world (*c*), what human reason (*b*) is in respect to the work of human art (*a*).

The first of these propositions is of the mythological order, addressed to the heart; the second, philosophical, engaging the head. Kant discusses the implication of the second of the two, as follows:

"Herewith the nature of the highest cause itself remains unknown to me; I only compare its known effect (namely, the constitution of the universe) and the rationality of this effect with the known effects of human reason, and therefore I call that highest cause a Reason, without thereby attributing to it as its proper quality, either the thing that I understand by this term in the case of man, or any other thing with which I am familiar." [2]

Indeed, as Kant has also argued, whereas the idea of a cause as prerequisite to any *effect* is a rational notion relevant to and confirmed by physical observations *within* the temporal field of phenomenal appearances, its application *a priori* to a supposed relationship between eternity (as First Cause) and temporality (as Created Effect) is but by analogy, and an imprecise analogy at that. For temporal effects succeed in time their "efficient" causes, whereas, since there never was a time when time was not, the "morphogenetic" relationship of eternity to time is not to be thought of as sequential. Moreover, eternity being by definition outside or beyond temporality, transcendent of all categories, whether of virtue or of reason (being and nonbeing, unity and multiplicity, love and justice, forgiveness and wrath), the term and concept "God" is itself but a metaphor of the unknowing mind, connotative, not only beyond itself, but beyond thought. So that all that can be said of it, whether as touching time or eternity, has to be in the way of an "as if" *(als ob):* philosophically and theologically (as Kant has just shown), through the analogy of a rationally inferred First Cause, and mythologically (as in his earlier example), in the way of a psychologically affective image transparent to transcendence.[3]

For example, at the opening of the Lord's Prayer ("Our Father, who art in Heaven..."), the invocation, "Our Father," is metaphorical, since the designated subject is not, in fact, a male parent, nor even a human being; yet its import is psychological, since the phrase suggests a relationship and system of human sentiments such as that of a child to its male parent, while there is evident, also, a transcendent, or metaphysical, connotation, in that the implied parent is not of this earth, and thus of time and space, but of eternity, in "Heaven," which is our popular term for the morphogenetic field.

An equivalent prayer could as well have been addressed to "Our Mother, who art within or beneath the earth." In fact, there have been many religions, and there may yet be many more, for which the preferred "as if," or "make believe," is of the child to its mother; and the sentiments evoked by this spiritual attitude have conduced to the appearances in many parts of the world of customs, arts, and manners of worship very different from those of the metaphorical child of a metaphysical father.

In the popular nightmare of history, where local mythic images are interpreted, not as metaphors, but as facts, there have been ferocious wars waged between the parties of such contrary manners of metaphoric representation. The Bible abounds in examples. And today (1984–85), in the

formerly charming little city of Beirut, the contending zealots of three differing inflections even of the same idea of a single paternal "God" are un-
loading bombs on each other.

One cannot but ask: What can such tribal literalism possibly contribute
but agony to such a world of intercultural, global prospects as that of our
present century? It all comes of misreading metaphors, taking denotation
for connotation, the messenger for the message; overloading the carrier,
consequently, with sentimentalized significance and throwing both life and
thought thereby off balance. To which the only generally recognized correction as yet proposed has been the no less wrongheaded one of dismissing
the metaphors as lies (which indeed they are, when so construed), thus
scrapping the whole dictionary of the language of the soul (this is a
metaphor) by which mankind has been elevated to interests beyond procre-
ation, economics, and "the greatest good of the greatest number."

Do I hear, coming as from somewhere that is nowhere, the frightening
sound of an Olympian laugh?

METAPHOR AS FACT AND FACT AS METAPHOR

Among the most widely known and (formerly) commonly understood
symbolic signs inherited from Bronze Age times by the high civilizations of
both the Occident and the Orient were the sun and moon: the latter, the
moon, which sheds its shadow to be born again, connoting the power of
life, as here engaged in the field of time, to throw off death—which is to
say, the power of life, as here embodied in each of us, to know itself as transcendent of carnality; with the sun, the light of which is unshadowed, recognized as the light and energy of consciousness disengaged from this field
of time, transcendent and eternal.

In the context of these symbolic assignments, the cycle of a single lunar
month has been compared, by analogy, to the term of a human lifetime,
with the fifteenth night, which is of the moon become full, equated with
the human adult's thirty-fifth year (in the reckoning of three-score years
and ten as the human norm).[4] On that very special evening there is a moment when the rising moon, having just emerged on the horizon, is directly
faced across the world, from the opposite horizon, by the setting sun.
Certain months of the year and the two, at this perfectly balanced moment,

are of equal light and the same size. By analogy, the confrontation has been likened to that in the midmoment of a lifetime when the light of consciousness reflected in the mind may be recognized, either suddenly or gradually, as identical with that typified metaphorically as of the sun. Whereupon, if the witness is prepared, there ensues a transfer of self-identification from the temporal, reflecting body to the sunlike, eviternal source, and one then knows oneself as consubstantial with what is of no time or place but universal and beyond death, yet incarnate in all beings everywhere and forever; so that as we again may read in the Upaniṣad: *tat tvam asi,* "thou art that." [5]

This is the realization connoted in the metaphor of the Virgin Birth, when in the mind and heart the ideal is conceived of a life lived, not for the primary economic and biological ends of survival, progeny, prosperity, and a little fun, but to a metaphysical end, intending values transcendent of historical survival. Teachers, accordingly, whose "kingdom is not of this world" (John 18:36), as well as heroic personages or legendary figures who have given themselves totally to great causes, may be represented in folk memory as of virgin births. The motif is of common occurrence in American Indian lore. In Greek mythology heroes begotten of Zeus are un-numbered. Even in the Old Testament there is a modified suggestion of the motif in Sarah's conception of Isaac at the age of ninety (Genesis 17:16–19, 18:9–15, 21:1–2); and again a suggestion hardly disguised in the chapter of the birth of Samson (Judges 13).

During the first five Christian centuries the question remained un-settled as to whether Mary had conceived *literally* of God or had normally given birth to a son who then had become endowed by God when, on being baptized in the Jordan, "he saw the heavens opened and the Spirit descending upon him like a dove; and a voice came from heaven, 'Thou art my beloved Son; with thee I am well pleased'" (Mark 1:11). It was only in the year A.D. 431, at the church council held in Ephesus (which at that time was the greatest temple-city in the Near East of the Great Goddess of Many Names: Artemis, Ishtar, Astarte, Anahit, Aphrodite, Isis, and so on) that the earthly mother, Mary, of the historical Jesus was authoritatively declared to have been literally *Theotókos* ("God-bearer," "mother of God").

The bishop Nestorius of Constantinople refused to accept this reification of the metaphor and was exiled to die in an Egyptian desert. However, a significant number of Christian communities (chiefly of Asia Minor and Syria) also refused and, emigrating to Persia, there established the seat of a "Nestorian" tradition, which by the end of the tenth century had become the representative Christianity of Central and East Asia, along the caravan routes and into China. In those parts of the Orient the well-known mythic metaphor of the Virgin Birth was not in this instance miraculized as a physical fact.

The historical fact of the Crucifixion, on the other hand, has been throughout the Christian centuries miraculized as the medium of "Salvation," with this latter term subject to a variety of interpretations. The founding myth has been, of course, that of Man's Fall by the Tree in the Garden (Genesis 3) and Salvation by virtue of the sacrifice of the God-Man Christ Jesus on the Tree of the Cross (Matthew 27:33–54; Mark 15:22–39; Luke 23:33–49; John 19:17–30), whereby a mythological Fall has become historicized as a prehistoric fact of c. 4004 or 3760 B.C., and a *historical* crucifixion, c. A.D. 30, mythologized as reparation for that Fall. The result has been a blend of history and mystery of such compelling fascination that both the psychological and the metaphysical connotations of the metaphoric symbols have been all but lost in the pathos of the screen.

Dispassionately analyzed, however, by way of comparative-mythological equations, the narrative opens readily to its archetypal revelation. For the biblical mythologem of *The Fall* is but a variant of the universally known *Separation of Heaven and Earth,* where the consciousness of an intelligible "Presence" informing all the transformations of the temporal shapes of the world is represented as having been in some way, at some moment, lost, with the mind and spirit of mankind then trapped in phenomenality alone. While the metaphor of *Salvation, Redemption,* or *At-one-ment,* is connotative simply of a restoration to the deluded mind of its original intuition of an identification of the features of time with eternal life; as appears, for example, in the words of Christ reported in the recently discovered Gnostic *Gospel According to Thomas:* "Cleave a piece of wood, I am there; lift up the stone and you will find me there" (Logion 77:26–27).[6] Or again: "The Kingdom of the Father is spread upon the earth and men do not see it" (Logion 113:17).[7] The relevant Sanskrit terms are, respectively, *māyā,* the formative power of delusion, and *bodhi,* illumination.

The Old Testament motif of the Promised Land, interpreted comparatively in this way, relieved of its ethnic associations and so revealed as a local variant of a mythological archetype known from many parts of the world, takes on a meaning very different from that of a divine mandate to conquer and occupy by military force an already populated area of the Near East. The very much later medieval idea of the Earthly Paradise is a variant of the same theme, representing a spiritual region, or condition of mind, wherein phenomenal forms are recognized as revelatory of transcendence. The Navaho of the North American Southwest identify every feature of the magnificent desert in which they dwell with an equivalent feature of their mythology: the coyotes, the various mountains, watercourses, frogs, serpents, rainbows, spiders, red ants, dragonflies, and so on—so that wherever they go and whatever they see, they are in mind of supporting powers. Likewise the Norse, who in the ninth century A.D. settled uninhabited Iceland, mythologized the raw landscape. *Land nám* ("land claiming or taking") was their technical term for this way of sanctifying a region, converting it thereby into an at once psychologically and metaphysically symbolic Holy Land.[8] And the Vedic Aryans on entering India, thirteenth century or so B.C., performed the same work upon the landscapes of the Indus Valley and Gangetic Plain.[9] "The Kingdom of the Father," we have just heard, "is spread upon the earth and men do not see it." *Land nám,* mythologization, has been the universally practiced method to bring this intelligible kingdom to view in the mind's eye. The Promised Land, therefore, is any landscape recognized as mythologically transparent, and the method of acquisition of such a territory is not by prosaic physical action, but poetically, by intelligence and the method of art; so that the human being should be dwelling in the two worlds simultaneously of the illuminated moon and the illuminating sun.

The festival of Easter, accordingly, is scheduled to coincide annually with the weekend of the first full moon following the solar spring equinox, thus calling to mind the old Bronze Age symbolic metaphor of its fifteenth night, when the moon, fully illuminated, is self-equaled to the sun. Jesus Christ, according to his legend, was about thirty-five years of age at the time of his crucifixion, as was also Guatama Buddha when he sat beneath the Bodhi Tree. The three metaphors are equivalent as alternative signs of the high mystical experience of an absorption of mortal appearance in immortal being; for which another historical figure of speech is the "End of the World."

METAPHORS OF PSYCHOLOGICAL TRANSFORMATION

In the normal course of a well-favored human lifetime the unfolding of the body's vital energy transpires through marked stages of transformation which in the pictographic lexicon of India's yogic schools are represented as controlled from separate spinal centers known as *cakras* (pronounced "chakras," meaning "circles, wheels"), also as *padmās* ("lotuses"). These are pictured and experienced as ranged in ascending order along an invisible spinal nerve or channel called *sushumnā* ("supremely blessed, rich in happiness")[10] (see Figure 3). The first and lowest of the series, described as situated between the anus and genitalia, is known as *mūlādhāra* ("root base") and identified as the motivating center of that simple, primal holding to life which is of infancy and early childhood. The body's urgency at this stage is to feeding and assimilating, which, as noticed in our introduction, is the precondition of all animal life, which can exist only by consuming lives. The second bioenergetic station, *svādhishthāna* (energy's "own, or especial, standing place"), is of sexuality, awakened during adolescence. And the third, known as *manipūra* ("city of the shining jewel"), at the level of the navel, is then of the will to power, mastery, and control, which in its healthy, positive aspect is of power achieved, with a sense of pride in responsibility; but in its morbid, negative form it appears as an insatiable will to conquer, plunder, and subjugate, converting everything and everybody within reach into one's own or one's like.

In the normal course of a lifetime, according to this yogic psychological schedule, the biological urges generated from these three pelvic spinal centers mature naturally in succession as the body develops through its first three and a half decades. These, and these alone, have supplied the motivations of historical man, his effective moral systems, and his nightmare of world history. They are the centers of the basic urges, furthermore, that mankind shares with the beasts—namely (1) to survive alive by feeding on other lives, (2) to generate offspring, and (3) to conquer and subdue. Unrestrained by any control system, these become devastating, as the history of the present century surely tells. For as declared in the Indian *Artha*

Śāstra, "Textbook on the Art of Winning": "When uncontrolled by virtue *(dharma)* and the big stick *(daṇḍa)*, men become wolves unto men." The elevation of the human will to aims transcendent of this bestial order of life requires, according to the yogic model, an awakening that will not be of the pelvic region, but of *cakra* 4, which is of the heart. The name of this transformative center, *anāhata,* has the curious meaning "not hit," which is interpreted as signifying "the Sound that is not made by any two things striking together." For every sound heard by the physical ear is of things rubbing or striking together. That of the voice, for example, is of breath on the vocal cords. The one sound not so made is the great tone, or hum *(śabda)*, of the creative energy *(māyā, śakti)* of which things are the manifestations, or epiphanies. And the intuitive recognition of this creative tone within a phenomenal form is what opens the heart to love. What before had been an "it" becomes then a "thou," alive with the tone of creation.

Figure 3. Figure seated in the yogic Lotus Position *(padmāsana),* illustrating the distribution of subtle Lotus Centers *(padmās,* or *cakras)* along the subtle spinal nerve or channel known as *sushumnā.* Two interlacing lateral nerves, *iḍā* (here dark) and *piṅgalā* (light), carry the vital breaths of the left, respectively, and right nostrils to the lowest center, where they may be brought to enter the *sushumnā.*

Each Lotus resounds to a special syllable and is endowed with symbolic features: 1. *mūlādhāra* (situated between the anus and genitals), of the element Earth, having four crimson petals and a yellow, rectangular interior bearing the sign of the syllable *lam;* 2. *svādhishṭhāna* (region of the genitals), of the element Water, with six vermilion petals and a white interior containing a crescent moon and the sign of the syllable *vam;* 3. *maṇipūra* (region of the navel), of the element Fire, with ten smoky-purple petals and a fiery triangle within, resounding to the syllable *ram.* These lowest three are centers of basic physical energies and urges.

4. *anāhata* (region of the heart), of the element Air (breath, *spiritus, prāṇa),* having twelve red petals and an interior showing a six-pointed star composed of two opposed triangles, one downward, the other upward turned, within which a golden *liṅgam-yonī* symbol connoting a subtle spiritual rapture resounds to the syllable *yam.*

Just below this Lotus of spiritual birth there is a minor center with eight petals, as a vestibule of meditation upon one's "chosen guardian deity" *(ishta-devatā).* There the

"Wish-fulfilling Tree" *(kalpataru)* is found, set upon a jewelled altar *(maṇipītha).*

The uppermost three centers are of increasingly sublimated spiritual realizations: 5. *viśuddha* (region of the larynx), of the element Space *(ākāsa,* often translated "ether"), having sixteen smoky-purple petals (same color as 3), a white triangle within (at 3 it was red, here clarified), and resounding to the syllable *ham.* This is the center of spiritual effort, leading to 6. *ājñā* (at the forehead, between and above the eyes: compare in Figure 1 the place of the *jinas,* the "Victors"). The Lotus here is of two petals, white and radiant as the moon, supporting a supreme vision of the Goddess, or of a God-with-Form, from which the tone is to be heard sounding of the syllable *OM;* beyond which there is, finally 7. the Lotus of a Thousand Petals, *sahasrāra,* inverted over the whole crown of the head, representing a rapture beyond any god known as of a name or form.

This is the way of seeing things that is of mythology and of what in chapter 3 is discussed as "The Way of Art": an awakening (metaphorically) to a New World (the Promised Land) and to Life in the Spirit (the Virgin Birth). In the way of nature one may experience, from time to time, glimpses of the world in this light—after the pelvic bioenergetic commitments have been honored and fulfilled, so that, freed from the dictatorship of the species, one is released to live as an individual (some little time, say, after the age of about thirty-five). The disciplines of yoga and devotional religion are meant to facilitate and ensure attainment of this revelation. However, as every chronicle of war and peace unquestionably demonstrates, it has simply not been within the power of our historical religions to open the hearts of congregations beyond their own recognized horizons: which at this historic moment is unfortunate, since (to repeat the argument of our introduction) with the populations of the planet now on the point of becoming one, there are in fact no more horizons beyond which to project upon aliens the malice of God's unsublimated product, historical man. Apparently, the words of Christ, "But I say to you, Love your enemies" (Matthew 5:44), have today to be taken seriously, even by monotheists.

The transformation of character that is prerequisite for living in the light of a transformed world is symbolized in the imagery of the yogic lotus ladder by a final triad of *cakras*—numbers 5, 6, and 7—which are of the head and mind pursuing aims and ends beyond range of the physical senses. The first of these, *viśuddha* ("cleansed, clarified, perfectly pure"), is pictured at the level of the larynx (the seat of abstract speech), and the work to be accomplished there is a clarification of the senses, to the end of Blake's already quoted dictum: "If the doors of perception were cleansed, every thing would appear to man as it is, infinite." The required method to this end is known as *the turning about of the energy*, which is to say, simply, an application of all the available malice and aggression of *cakra* 3, not outward to the correction of the world, but inward, upon oneself; as in Jesus' thought: not removing the mote from one's brother's eye, but casting out the beam from one's own (Matthew 7:3–5, abridged). The Indian pictorial metaphor is of a wrathful deity in demonic form, wearing necklaces of severed heads, kilts of severed arms and legs, flourishing weapons and trampling down human shapes underfoot. This demon is a manifestation of one's own impulse to aggression turned back on oneself, the vanquished shapes underfoot representing attachment to physical desires and the fear of physical death.

The next and last two stages of the ascending lotus series are then of the two ways of experiencing what is known as "God," either as "with form" or as "without." The lotus at *cakra* 6, known as *ājñā* ("authority, order, unlimited power, command"), is situated within the head, above, behind, and between the eyes. There it is that the radiant image of one's *idea* of "God" is beheld, while at *cakra* 7, *sahasrāra* (the lotus, "thousand petaled")—which is represented as an inverted corolla covering the crown of the head, "bright with the brightness of ten million suns"—both the beheld image and the beholding mind dissolve together in a blaze that is at once of nonbeing and of being.

In a sermon entitled "Riddance," the great Dominican mystic, Meister Eckhart (c. 1260–1328), declared; "Man's last and highest leave-taking is leaving God for God." [11] And the Indian saint Ramakrishna (1836–1886) is reported to have remarked, "At the break of day He disappears into the secret chamber of His House." [12] Dante (1265–1321), in the culminating canto of his poetical account of his own spiritual ascent in vision up the metaphorical scale, from Hell, through Purgatory and the ranges of Heaven, to the Beatific Vision beheld in a blaze of eternal light, declares that there, within the profound subsistence of that light, there appeared, besides the triune image of his God, three circles of three colors and one magnitude. And "I wished to see," he states, "how the image conformed to the circle and how it has its place therein; but my own wings were not sufficient for that, save that my mind was smitten by a flash wherein its wish came to it." [13]

There is a Hindu tantric saying, *nādevo devam arcayet,* "by none but a god shall a god be worshiped." The deity of one's worship is a function of one's own state of mind. But it also is a product of one's culture. Catholic nuns do not have visions of the Buddha, nor do Buddhist nuns have visions of Christ. Ineluctably, the image of any god beheld—whether interpreted as beheld in heaven or as beheld at *cakra* 6—will be of a local ethnic idea historically conditioned, a metaphor, therefore, and thus to be recognized as transparent to transcendence. Remaining fixed to its name and form, whether with simple faith or in saintly vision, is therefore to remain in mind historically bound and attached to an appearance.

In the vocabulary of yoga, the two modes of realization, at *cakra* 6 and *cakra* 7, are termed, respectively, *saguṇa brahman* (the "qualified absolute") and *nirguṇa brahman* (the "unqualified absolute"), while the two related orders of meditation are, respectively, *savikalpa samādhi* ("discriminating absorption") and *nirvikalpa samādhi* ("undifferentiated absorption"). "But this," said Ramakrishna in discussion of the latter, "is an extremely difficult path. To one who follows it even the divine play in the world becomes like a dream and appears unreal; his 'I' also vanishes. The followers of this path do not accept the Divine Incarnation. It is a very difficult path. The lovers of God should not hear much of such reasoning."[14]

THRESHOLD FIGURES

Thus at the threshold of the passage from time to eternity, which is in fact the plane of reference of the metaphors of myth, the unmitigated yogic way (according to Ramakrishna) is to lose oneself, together with the world, in transcendence, following to the end the metaphysical connotations of the icons of devotion, disengaging altogether from their psychological hold, to the loss of the psyche itself; whereas the more temperate, properly devotional way is to hold in faithful love to the icons. For, as threshold figures, these are of the two worlds at once: temporal in the human appeal of their pictured denotations, while by connotation opening to eternity.

"Once upon a time," said Ramakrishna one evening to his friends, "a *sannyāsī* [mendicant monk] entered the temple of Jagganāth. As he looked at the holy image he debated within himself whether God had a form or was formless. He passed his staff from left to right to feel whether it touched the image. The staff touched nothing. He understood that there was no image before him; he concluded that God was formless. Next he passed the staff from right to left. It touched the image. The *sannyāsī* understood that God had form. Thus he realized that God has form and, again, is formless."[15]

"Brahman, Existence-Knowledge-Bliss Absolute," Ramakrishna continued, "is like a shoreless ocean. In the ocean visible blocks of ice are formed here and there by intense cold. Similarly, under the cooling influence, so to speak, of the devotion *[bhakti]* of its worshipers, the Infinite transforms Itself into the finite and appears before the worshiper as God with form. That is to say, God reveals Himself to His devotees as an embodied Person. Again, as, on the rising of the sun, the ice in the ocean melts away, so, on the awakening of Knowledge *[jñāna]*, the embodied God melts back into the infinite and formless Brahman.... Therefore people compare the love of God to the cooling light of the moon, and knowledge to the burning rays of the sun."[16]

In terms of the ascent of the yogic lotus ladder, the ultimate aim of any worshiper of a God with form must be to come to rest forever (as at *cakra* 6) in an eviternal heaven, "tasting the ambrosial juice" of bliss in the presence of the worshiped form; whereas a fully aspiring mystic will be making every effort to pass through and beyond that moonlike reflecting image to extinction (at *cakra* 7) in the full light of the sun. "In that state," said Ramakrishna, "reasoning stops altogether and man becomes mute.... A salt doll once went to measure the depths of the ocean.... No sooner did it get into the ocean than it melted. Now who was there to report the ocean's depth?"[17]

There is, however, a third position, typified in the Mahāyāna Buddhist ideal of the Bodhisattva, whose "being or nature" *(sattva)* is "enlightenment" *(bodhi),* and who yet with unquenched "compassion" *(karuṇā)* for his or her fellow creatures has either remained in or returned to this suffering world, to teach. Such a one was Ramakrishna himself. Such a one is the Dalai Lama. An equivalent understanding is to be recognized in the figure of Christ Crucified, "who," as we read in St. Paul to the Philippians, "though he was in the form of God, did not count equality with God a thing to be grasped [or clung to[18]], but emptied himself, taking the form of a servant, being born in the likeness of men. And being found in human form he humbled himself and became obedient unto death, even death on a cross."

In Albrecht Dürer's woodcuts of scenes of the Crucifixion (see Figure 4), disks of the sun and moon appear in the upper left and right corners. Likewise, in the upper left and right corners of Tibetan processional banners representing Bodhisattvas, disks of the sun and moon may appear, for the same reason. These are explicit references to that moment, already noted (see page 31), of the moon rising full on its fifteenth night, confronting with equal radiance the sun setting at that moment on the opposite horizon: the moon not quenched in solar light, but, fully illuminated, self-equaling.

Figure 4. Albrecht Dürer, *The Great Crucifixion.* Woodcut. 22$\frac{1}{2}$ x 15$\frac{3}{4}$ inches, from The Great Passion Series. A.D. 1498 (book editions, from 1511).

    Upper left, sun of the spring equinox; upper right, full moon of Easter.

For these are threshold forms at the interface of time and eternity. Read in one direction, they symbolize the passage of the light of consciousness from engagement in the field of birth and death (the lunar body, which dies) to identification with an immortal source, "which neither is born, nor does it ever die; nor, having once been will it cease to be. Unborn, eternal, perpetual and primeval, it is not slain when the body is slain" (Bhagavad Gītā 2:20). Whereas, read in the opposite sense, the figures represent (as in the passage quoted from Paul to the Philippians) the willing participation in the sorrows of space-time of one who, though in the knowledge of himself as of the nature of immortal bliss, yet voluntarily, as an avatar (Sanskrit, *avatāra,* from *ava-,* "down," plus *tarati,* "he passes across or over") joyfully engages in the fragmentation of life in Time. There is a form of the crucifix known as "Christ Triumphant," where the figure of the Savior is shown not broken, bleeding, naked, and with head dropped to the side, but with head erect, eyes open, body clothed, and arms outstretched as though willingly "thus come" *(tathāgata),* as the very image of a Bodhisattva in whom the agony of time and the rapture of eternity are disclosed as one and the same.

Sun and moon in the practiced disciplines of the yoga of expanding consciousness are associated psychophysiologically with two subtle nerves, or channels, of "vital energy" *(prāṇik),* known as *nāḍīs,* "stems or tubes," which are related to the breathing and breaths of the right, respectively, and left nostrils. These descend along the central spinal cord to right and to left of the *sushumnā,* ending with it together at the *mūlādhāra, cakra* 1, which is accordingly known as *Yuktatriveṇī,* "Three River Junction," this being an allegorical reference, in the way of a geographical *land nám* identification, to the mythological junction at Allahabad of the Jumna, Ganges, and (to mortal eyes invisible river) Sarasvati.[19]

The right nerve, known as *piṅgalā* ("tawny, reddish brown"), is red (in Figure 3, unshaded). The breath that it carries from the right nostril to the *mūlādhāra* is of solar energy—"masculine," fiery, poisonous, and deadly; for the sun, as Ramakrishna has told, is of consciousness absolute and eternal, disengaged from space-time and temporal life. It is a blaze of sheer spirit, whose full force is more than corporeal life can stand. In contrast, the left nerve, known as *iḍā* ("refreshment, poured libation, revivifying draft"), is pale yellowish or white (shaded in Figure 3), and the breath that it carries from the left nostril down to the *mūlādhāra* is of lunar energy, associated with moisture, "feminine," cooling and refreshing as dew. The moon, ever dying and self-renewed, is symbolic of consciousness incarnate in all living beings, suffering in each the pains of desire for the passing gratifications of temporal life, subject in each to death, and yet through death's progeny renewed. It is thus the celestial sign of the necessity of sacrifice; for with each giving of itself to death, lunar life (as distinguished from the term of a single lunation) is sustained.

Life temporal and eternal, attachment to the world and disengagement from the world: as usually regarded, these are opposed terms. In the imagery of moon and sun, however, the two are brought together, since the light of the moon is but solar light reflected. Likewise, by analogy, our body's life is eternal life, reflected, and our body's consciousness, eternal consciousness, only modified by the limitations of our mind's logical manner of dualistic thinking. Break those limitations (so runs the argument of yoga) and the mind regains possession of Original Knowledge: the salt doll walks into the ocean.

The practical method employed to the achievement of this end is indeed strange. It is known as *prāṇāyāma*, "disciplined control *(yāma)* of the breath *(prāṇa;* Latin, *spiritus).*" But the sense of it becomes obvious, once the assignments are recognized of mortality and immortality to the breaths of the left, respectively, and right nostrils.

The yogi, seated in the "lotus position" *(padmāsana)*, legs crossed, spine erect, eyes focused to a plane at about the distance to the point of the nose (not to be distracted by anything beyond that plane), begins by inhaling, first, through the right nostril, imagining solar energy as thus being brought into the "fiery" nerve, *piṅgalā*, down to the *mūlādhāra*. Holding the lungs full for a determined time, experiencing solar energy as pervading the whole body, the yogi then exhales through the left nostril, thus bringing breath of the lunar aspect up through *iḍā* and out into the world. The next inhalation will be through the left nostril, down through *iḍā* to the *mūlādhāra;* holding; and exhaling then through *piṅgalā;* and so on and on.

This continuing through hours without end for days, for months, or for years, at some point the body and mind together become fundamentally aware and convinced that *the energy by which the body is pervaded is the same as that which illuminates the world and maintains alive all beings,* the two breaths being the same: which is the moment of an awakening of the body itself to its inherent spirituality and the beginning of the ascent of *prāṇa* up the central nerve or channel, the *sushumnā*.[20] Ramakrishna has described the actual sensation of the rising current:

"Sometimes the Spiritual Current rises through the spine, crawling like an ant. Sometimes, in *samādhi,* the soul swims joyfully in the ocean of divine ecstasy, like a fish. Sometimes, when I lie down on my side, I feel the Spiritual Current pushing me like a monkey and playing with me joyfully. I remain still. That Current, like a monkey, suddenly with one jump reaches the *sahasrāra.* That is why you see me jump with a start. Sometimes, again, the Spiritual Current rises like a bird hopping from one branch to another. The place where it rests feels like fire.... Sometimes the Spiritual Current moves up like a snake. Going in a zigzag way, at last it reaches the head and I go into *samādhi.* A man's spiritual consciousness is not awakened unless his *kuṇḍalinī* is aroused."[21]

Kuṇḍalinī (kuṇḍalin, "circular, annulate, coiled"; *kuṇḍalinī,* a feminine noun meaning "serpent"): *kuṇḍalinī* is *essential spiritual energy* pictured as a coiled white serpent asleep in the *mūlādhāra* of each of us. Serpents shed their skins, as the moon its shadow, to be as it were reborn. Symbolically, therefore, they are terrestrial counterparts, by analogy, of the heavenly moon, connoting, like the moon, the light of immortal consciousness engaged, even trapped, in the field of space-time. The continuous flashing of their fiery forked tongues testifies to the trapped light within them. Hence, the uncoiling "Serpent Power," *kuṇḍalinī,* ascending the *sushumnā* to unite at the crown of our head with the lotus "Thousand Petaled," *sahasrāra,* "bright with the brightness of ten million suns," is equivalent—again by analogy—to the moon approaching its fifteenth night, when its light will match that of the sun. *Kuṇḍalinī* and *sahasrāra* therewith unite as one: which is to say (to change the metaphor), a salt doll once walked into the ocean.

Figure 5. Damaged faience seal showing a figure in a classic yoga posture (*mūlaban-dhāsana)*, venerated by human beings and serpents; reverse, characters of an undeciphered script. Indus Valley Civilization, c. 2300–c. 1750 B.C.

Figure 6. Three-faced deity in a classic yoga posture *(mūlabandhāsana)* among animals; clockwise, left to right: tiger, elephant, rhinoceros, and water buffalo. Faience seal. Indus Valley Civilization, c. 2300–c. 1750 B.C.

That extreme psychophysiological exercises of this highly sophisticated and effective, spiritually transformative degree have been practiced in India for at least four thousand years, we know from the evidence of a number of engraved stamp seals from the period of the Indus Valley Civilization, c. 2000 B.C., featuring figures seated in a classic yoga posture known as *mūlabandhāsana,* which is still in practice (see Figures 5 and 6). The serpents rising at either hand of one of these seated figures strongly suggest the two lateral channels, *iḍā* and *piṅgalā,* with the yogi in the place of the *sushumnā.* The figure on the other seal here illustrated is distinctly a divinity of a type suggesting Śiva, who in Hindu thought is the principal god associated with yoga. In the justly celebrated, magnificent image of Śiva the Great Lord in the cave temple of Elephanta, Bombay (eighth century A.D.), the god is represented with three faces: proper right, a male profile (compare *piṅgalā); proper* left, a female profile *(iḍā);* and in the center a glorious countenance, full face, reflecting eternity *(sushumnā).* The tiny Indus Valley image has also (apparently) three faces. Moreover, the prime symbol of Śiva is the *liṅgam* (erect phallus), symbolic of his creative energy ever pouring into the cosmic womb *(yonī)* of the world-mother, Māyā-Śakti-Devī, while his emblematic weapon is the trident *(triśūla),* which is already suggested in the meditating triune god's extraordinary headdress. Finally, the little figure is surrounded by four animals (possibly of the four directions), a tiger, an elephant, a rhinoceros, and a water buffalo. One cannot but think of representations in European medieval art of Christ of the Second Coming, surrounded by four figures symbolizing the evangelists, Matthew, Mark, Luke, and John—namely, a man, a lion, a bull, and an eagle, which are actually the four zodiacal signs of the solstices and equinoxes of the calendar of the Taurian age, c. 2000 B.C., respectively, the Water Bearer of the winter solstice of that time, Lion of the summer solstice, Bull of the spring equinox, and Eagle (later, Scorpion) of the autumnal equinox. These are the same four that appear combined in the chimeric forms of those great Assyrian gate-guarding cherubim from the palace at Nimrud of Ashurnasirpal II (ruled 883–859 B.C.), which are compounded of the head of a man, wings of an eagle, body of a bull, and feet of a lion (see Figure 7).

Figure 7. Portal guardian from the palace of Ashurnasirpal II at Nimrud, Assyria, 883–859 B.C. Limestone. Height 11 feet 6 inches.

This chimeral cherub combines the body of a bull, feet of a lion, wings and breast of an eagle, and a human head wearing a miter with six horns. These are features suggesting the four zodiacal signs of the spring and autumn equinoxes, summer and winter solstices, as they appeared when, not Aries, but Taurus was the vernal equinoctial sign; namely: Taurus, Leo, an Eagle (which later became Scorpio, see Figure 10), and Aquarius. So combined, these four brought together in one symbolic form the quarters of that whole revolving screen of the sky, beyond and behind which the god Ashur resided—as Ashurnasirpal, his vicar on earth, beyond and behind the wall and portal protected by this Taurian cherub. In the prophet Ezekiel's vision, late sixth century B.C., the same four beasts were seen in the faces of the "creatures " before God's throne (Ezekiel 1:5–11; also 10:9–14), and in Christian iconography, they again appear as signs of the Evangelists.

Additional thoughts which come to mind are of Dante's representation of Satan in the *Inferno* (Canto XXXIV, lines 28–69) with three faces: "one in front," we read, "and it was red, and the other two joined to this just over the middle of each shoulder, and all were joined at the crown. The right one seemed between white and yellow, and the left one was such in appearance as are those who come from whence the Nile descends."[22] Red, black, and pale yellow, the faces represented for Dante Impotence, Ignorance, and Hate, respectively, as direct negatives of the attributes of the Father, Son, and Holy Spirit, which are namely, Power, Wisdom, and Love (see Canto III, lines 5–6). Compare with this, Ramakrishna's attribution to the Absolute of "Existence, Knowledge, and Bliss": *sac-cid-ānanda brahman* (see page 40). I think, also, in this connection of Calvary's three crosses: one, of the crucified thief who would ascend to heaven (Luke 23:39–43), the other, of him who would descend to hell; and the cross between, of the Savior.

Of relevance, too, is the persistent ophitic tradition (Greek *ophis,* "serpent") of Christ in the image of a serpent: not only in illustration of the Savior's words to Nicodemus the Pharisee, likening himself to the serpent of bronze elevated by Moses in the wilderness (Numbers 21:5–9), but also in the Gnostic sense of an association of the messenger of salvation with the idea of the serpent in the Garden of Eden, who according to this way of inverting the orthodox interpretation, had been the first to attempt to release mankind from bondage to an unknowing god who had identified himself with the Absolute and thus blocked the way to the tree of eternal life. (See Figure 8.)

In Buddhist temple art, and indeed in temple art generally, the entrances to sacred precincts are represented as attended by two gate, or threshold, guardians *(dvarāpāla),* which are frequently of threatening mien, with lifted weapons and blazing eyes, one with his mouth open, the other with his mouth shut (see Figure 9). These are counterparts of the cherubim that Yahweh placed "at the east of the garden of Eden, and a flaming sword which turned every way, to guard the way to the tree of life" (Genesis 3:22–24). (See again Figure 7.) In the Navaho sand painting reproduced in Figure 15 (on page 71), the same two are termed "Spirit Bringers" *(ethkaynaáshi),* where they stand as openers of the way into and through a sacred area that in structure and sense corresponds remarkably to what we are told of the stages of the *sushumnā.*

Figure 8. "The Serpent Lifted Up." Thaler struck by the goldsmith Hieronymus Magdeburger. Annaberg, Germany. A.D. sixteenth century.

Text: "And as Moses lifted up the serpent in the wilderness [Numbers 21:5–91], so must the Son of Man be lifted up; that whoever believes in him may have eternal life" (John 3:15).

In Tantric thought these figures are to be understood as located in the *mūlādhāra,* standing as personifications of the lunar and solar breaths at either side of the gate of the *sushumnā,* at the openings, respectively, of the *iḍā* and *piṅgalā* nerves. For it is there, as we recall, at *Yuktatriveṇī,* "The Meeting Place of Three Rivers," that the differentiated lunar and solar energies at last blend to a single fire, which then, like a blast, ascends with the awakened *kuṇḍalinī* into and along the central way. Until this fusion of the two breaths occurs, the central portal remains closed. The embodied *lunar* consciousness of the practicing individual must first, that is to say, be experienced as in fact the same as the universal *solar* consciousness by which all beings are energized and given light. Otherwise the mind will either remain locked in materiality, imagining the body and its experience to be of matter alone, or fly rapt away on some supernatural fancy, as though (the universe being of matter alone) soul or spirit should be sought somewhere else.

Figure 9. *Kongō-rikishi* (Sanskrit, *Vajrapāṇi,* "Thunderbolt Handler"), Giant Threshold Guardians housed at opposite sides of the portal of The Great South Gate before Tōdaiji, Temple of the Great Sun Buddha, Mahāvairochana (Japanese, Dainichi-nyorai). Nara, Japan. Wood. Height, 26 feet, 6 inches. A.D. 1203.

Figure 10. Design from the Libation Cup of King Gudea of Lagash, Sumer, c. 2000 B.C.

Two cherubim, or "lion birds" with scorpion tails, draw back the portals of a shrine to reveal a manifestation of the Sumero-Akkadian serpent-god Ningishzida in dual aspect, as a pair of copulating vipers interlaced along a staff. A relationship is evident, on the one hand, to the caduceus of Greek Hermes, guide of souls to the knowledge of eternal life and patron of hermetic arts, and on the other hand, to the Indian "Serpent Power" in the *sushumnā* with its two interlacing lateral nerves, as illustrated in Figure 3. The Sumerian date, c. 2000 B.C., matches that of the two Indus Valley seals of Figures 5 and 6.

A simple Buddhist interpretation of the two threatening figures at the portal to immortality would be as representing, not the obstructing will of an external god, but the inhibiting attachment of the human will itself to physical mortality in obsessive fear of physical death. For in this view immortality is already ours. Only the mind's attachment to mortal aims has deprived us of this knowledge. Physical desire and fear (the two temptations overcome by Prince Gautama Shakyamuni on the night of his attainment of Buddhahood) are all that are debarring us from the Garden in which, ironically, we already dwell; for in this tradition there never was an Exile, only a mistaken focus of mind; as Jesus also is reported to have declared (in the recently discovered and translated Gnostic Gospel of Thomas): "The Kingdom is within you" (Logion 3), and again, "The Kingdom of the Father is spread upon the earth and men do not see it" (Logion 113). [23]

And so, indeed, it does appear that anyone viewing with unprejudiced eye the religions of mankind must recognize mythic themes at every hand that are shared, though differently interpreted, among the peoples of this planet. James G. Frazer, in *The Golden Bough,* thought to explain such correspondences simply as "the effect of similar causes acting alike on the similar constitution of the human mind in different countries and under different skies." [24] Bastian, as we have seen, characterized them as "elementary ideas," and C. G. Jung, as we have also remarked, proposed his theory of "archetypes of the unconscious."

There are, however, instances that cannot be so readily interpreted in purely psychological terms, where, as for example in the matter of our present interest, a structured constellation of ideas, images, and related exercises yielding transformational experiences will have appeared over an extensive historical field, here and there in damaged condition perhaps, or creatively modified, yet unmistakably of one originating structure.

For it is evident that knowledge of what is known today in India as the *kuṇḍalinī* was not in ancient times confined to the Indus Valley Civilization. From nearby Mesopotamia of the same date, c. 2000 B.C., there is an ornamented Sumerian ritual vessel, known as the Libation Vase of King Gudea of Lagash, upon which, in high relief, the mystery scene appears of two cherubim, or Lion Birds, attending the portal of a shrine to the great Mesopotamian serpent-god Ningishzida under the aspect of a pair of copulating vipers (see Figure 10). They are entwined about an axial rod in such a way as to suggest both the caduceus of classical Hermes (guide of souls to the knowledge of eternal life) and the seven spinal centers of the *sushumnā*. There is from Egypt, somewhat later, 1405–1367 B.C. (nineteenth dynasty), from a Theban copy of the *Book of the Dead,* an exceptional representation of the standard Egyptian judgment scene of the weighing of the heart of the deceased against a feather, where the pole is marked by seven distinct nodules below the balance beam and an eighth above it (see Figure 11). The nose of Osiris's monstrous watchdog, the Swallower (a mixture of crocodile, hippopotamus, and lion, who is to swallow the soul if the heart is heavier than the feather), cuts directly across the pole between its third and fourth nodules (read, third and fourth *cakras*), which, furthermore, is exactly the level of a platform, across the way, supporting a seated baboon (the animal symbolic of Thoth, Egyptian counterpart of the Greek Hermes). In terms of the *kuṇḍalinī* the message could hardly be clearer; namely, if the aims of the deceased in life were no higher than those of *cakra* 3, the Swallower claims the soul; whereas, if the "sound not made by any two things striking together" had been heard (at *cakra* 4) and heeded in the lifetime, Thoth will conduct the blessed soul (light as a feather) to Osiris's throne by the Waters of Eternal Life. [25]

There is in the Musée Guimet, in Paris, from China of the Chou dynasty, c. 1027–256 B.C., a coiled bronze serpent (see Figure 12) showing just three and one-half turns, which, to me at least, very strongly suggests the *kuṇḍalinī* in the *mūlādhāra*. [26] And at the opposite margin of the vast Eurasian common-culture field, in Ireland, ninth century A.D., not only were the enigmatic illuminations of the Book of Kells made alive with symbolic serpents (most remarkably, the so-called *Tunc*-page, illustrating Matthew 27:38: *tunc crucifixerant cum eo duos latrones,* "then there were crucified with him two thieves"), but also, on the side of an immense stone cross of the same pre-Gothic Christian period—the "Cross of [the Abbot] Muiredach," at Monasterboice (in Louth)—there was engraved in high relief an astonishing panel (see Figure 13) known as *Dextra Dei,* the "Right Hand of God," in which two interlacing serpents appear, one heading downward, the other upward, enframing three human heads in ascending series, with a human right hand above, reaching to the center of a crowning, halolike, ornamented disk. [27] If this is not an explicit reference to the top four states of an ascent of the *sushumnā*, the sense of such an appearance

Figure 11. Egyptian scene of the weighing of the heart of the deceased against a feather symbolic of Maat, goddess of the moral order of the universe. Papyrus illumination from *The Book of the Dead of Kenna*. XIX Dynasty (Thebes), between 1405 and 1367 B.C.

Exceptional here is the series of seven large nodules along the pole, up to the beam. (Compare the seven Lotus Centers in Figure 3.) The composite animal, lower left, known as the "Swallower," is there to consume anyone whose heart is found heavier than the feather. His long snout cuts across the pole between Nodules 3 and 4. (Compare in Figure 3 the connotations of the Lotus Centers 1, 2, and 3, as against 4.) The nose points directly to the level of the platform on which the god Thoth (Egyptian counterpart of Hermes, guide of souls to the knowledge of eternal life) in his baboon form (baboons, it is said, greet with a barking chorus the rising sun) adjusts the critical beam. Thus, whereas the "Swallower" stands for the qualities of Nodules 1, 2, and 3, the god Thoth (often represented as an ibis) adjudicates on those above. An eighth nodule appears above the beam, suggesting the possibility of a sphere of timeless consciousness to become known to the embalmed mummy. (Compare in Figure 1 the place of the Jaina "Victors" above the eyebrows of the universal goddess.)

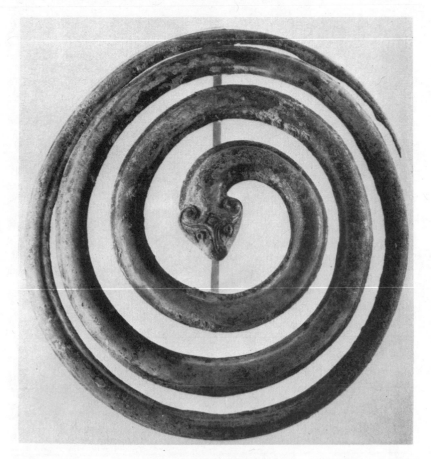

Figure 12. Coiled serpent. Bronze. China. Chou dynasty, Period of the Warring States, c. 500–250 B.C.

Showing exactly three and a half turns, this bronze serpent may be evidence already from pre-Buddhist China of an original knowledge in some way related to the much later tantric development in India, for the metaphorical coiled serpent said to be sleeping in the *mūlādhāra* is described as of three and a half turns.

on a Christian monument commemorating the Crucifixion remains to be explained. Indeed, in consideration of the fact that one of the major Christian philosophers of the period was the Irish Neoplatonist John Scotus Erigena (c. 810–877), whose principal work, *De divisione naturae,* suffered condemnation by the church because of its implication of pantheism, one may even suspect that covert Gnostic connotations may underlie much, if

Figure 13. *Dextra Dei,* "The Right Hand of God." Symbolic design from the side of a monumental stone cross in Ireland. Cross of the [Abbot] Muiredach, Monasterboice (Louth), A.D. tenth century.

not all, of the recondite Irish-monastic symbolic art of that formerly Druidic province of the Christian mission. The Irish abbots were still reading and translating Greek when the learning of the rest of Europe had been obliterated by the Goths, Vandals, Anglo-Saxons, and other pagan barbarians of the period of Rome's collapse. Certain peculiarities of their liturgies derived from a once universal Greek rite. And among the anchorites of the period, of whom apparently there were many, such extreme austerities were practiced as in later days were to be hardly known outside of Tibet; as, for example, that of "enclosure," retirement to a small stone cell "so low and narrow that a tall man could not lie full length," to remain there for life.[28] There can be no question that all the conditions were there present for an understanding both through learning and through experience of the spiritual connotations of the metaphors of the Christian faith, such as appears to have been lost to the rest of Europe (and finally to Ireland as well) during the centuries, first of pagan and then of ecclesiastical violence that followed upon the collapse of the already Christianized Roman Empire.

All of which suggests a number of possibly unanswerable questions relevant to the formation and manner of dispersal of such a distinct constellation of symbolic motifs as that which in India has been linked for the past four thousand years to the practice and actual experiences of yoga.

For it is evident, even from the brief series of examples that I have just now cited, that the temporal and geographical range of recognition of certain of the structuring elements of this distinct constellation is enormous. The earliest evidences—from the valleys of the Indus, Tigris-Euphrates, and Nile—point back to a period antecedent to the entry on the historical stage of the patriarchal Semitic and Indo-European warrior tribes. That Egyptian feather against which the heart of the deceased was to be weighed was an ostrich feather symbolic of the goddess Maat, as a personification of the cosmic order and its natural laws, to which both the social order and the order of an individual lifetime were required to conform—in contrast to the later, Zoroastrian-Judeo-Christian-Islamic-Marxist notion of nature as either "fallen" or indifferent and of society (the interests of the local cultural monad) as the ultimate determinant of and criterion for what is right and what wrong. The Indian idea of *dharma* (virtue in the performance of duty) and Chinese of the *tao* (the unitary first principle from which all order, change, and propriety in action spring) are alike derived from the same prehistoric background as the ancient Egyptian idea of the goddess Maat. And the structuring realization out of which these equivalent ideas arose was of a society and its members as equally products of nature—to be held in accord with nature by means of metaphorical disciplines, social and psychological, intending harmonization of the individual will with the general will and thereby with the will in nature. This is the idea already recognized in the Mesopotamian number 43,200 and its transformations (see pages 9–12), correlating, as of one measure, the cycles of the celestial spheres, periods of historic time, and pulsations of the human heart. Sir John Woodroffe (Arthur Avalon) adds that in the Indian yogic schools it is held that all living beings exhale and inhale 21,600 times a day:[29] 21,600 x 2 = 43,200.

In such a context, since the macrocosm (order of the universe), microcosm (order of the individual), and mesocosm (order of the attuned society) are equivalent, the social ideals and moral principles by which the individual is constrained to his group are conceived to be, finally, of his own nature. And for the same reason, the visionary realizations of the yogi in solitude would be of the psychological sources out of which the mesocosmic order of his mythologically grounded cultural monad originated. There is not, therefore, in this ancient manner of understanding man in relation to his universe, anything like those tensions of conflicting aims and values which the late Daisetz T. Suzuki remarked in our own biblically inspired, occidental way of relating to "nature" and the "spirit" as a pair of opposites: "Nature [here] is something hostile to Man and drags him down when he is struggling to reach God," Suzuki remarked. And he quoted: "'The spirit is willing but the flesh is weak' [Matthew 26:41]. Man is against God, Nature is against God, and Man and Nature are against each other. God's own likeness (Man), God's own creation (Nature) and God himself—all three are at war."[30]

At what time and in what place or places, then, did the great Eurasian constellation originate of those macro-micro-mesocosmic metaphors, ritualized devotions addressed to the same, and psychophysiological exercises reconfirming them, of which the Indian gurus, Tibetan rimpoches, and Japanese Zen masters are the inheritors? The evidences so far considered, from India, Mesopotamia, and Egypt, suggest some time and place within the period and region of the Late Neolithic and Early Bronze Age civilizations of the Near and Middle East, say c. 3500–2500 B.C. The problem is complicated, however, by such tokens from Native America as, for example, the Navaho sand painting already noticed, where the imagery and connotations so perfectly match those of the ascent of the *sushumnā* that if the painting had come from Tibet, instead of from New Mexico, an immediate connection could be assumed without hesitation.

My own realization that there was a problem here to be recognized occurred about forty years ago, when I was preparing for publication by the Bollingen Foundation a series of pollen paintings and their associated myth that had been received from an old Navaho medicine man, Jeff King (who in 1964 died at about the age of 110). Jeff King had declared that his paintings were derived "from a cave on the east slope of a certain mountain," which he had first visited in boyhood and could visit again whenever he wished to refresh his memory of the paintings. "Outside the cave," he said, "was a stone carving of two snakes intertwined, the heads facing east and west." Since his last visit, however, the serpent monument had been underwashed by water and had collapsed, so that it was now no more. [31] One hardly knows what to think of such a story. A stone carving in New Mexico? A form of Hermes's caduceus with the heads facing east and west instead of toward each other? My skepticism became qualified when I discovered among a series of figures reproduced from the pre-Columbian Codex Fejérváry-Mayer (now preserved in Liverpool, England) an example of just such a modified caduceus as Jeff King had described (see Figure 14). [32] Whether his stone carving had been of hard rock or of his own imagination, therefore, the form of it, as it now appeared, was traditional. From what source, however, the tradition?

In the 1950s R. Gordon Wasson's investigations of the Mexican pre-Columbian mushroom cult (in collaboration with Albert Hofmann, the Swiss chemist renowned for his discovery of LSD in 1943) established beyond question the prominence of hallucinogens in the religious exercises of the whole Mayan-Aztec culture field. The same investigators in conjunction with the classicist, Carl A. P. Ruck, have lately revealed the likelihood of the influence of a hallucinogen (ergot of barley) in the Greek mysteries of Eleusis. [33] Already in 1968, Wasson published his disclosure of the mysterious Vedic sacramental, Soma, as probably a product of the mushroom *Amanita*

Figure 14. Altar of the Caduceus. Pre-Columbian Aztec. Codex Fejérváry-Mayer, A.D. fifteenth century.

muscaria (fly agaric).[34] Aldous Huxley's *The Doors of Perception* (1954), describing his own visionary experiences under the influence of mescaline, opened the way to a popular appreciation of the ability of hallucinogens to render perceptions of a quasi- or even truly mystical profundity. There can be no doubt today that through the use of such sacramentals revelations indistinguishable from some of those reported of yoga have been experienced. Nor can there be any doubt that the source of the revelations is the psyche of the practitioner—the unconscious, that is to say. They are revelations, that is to say further, of the archetypes of the collective unconscious, elementary ideas *a priori* of the species *Homo sapiens sapiens,* such as may appear spontaneously no matter where.

Returning to an anthropological vocabulary, we may then feel safe in suggesting that such symbols as the caduceus might well have appeared in India, Greece, Ireland, and New Mexico independently, by "parallelism," out of the common ground of what C. G. Jung has termed the collective unconscious. The problem that confronts us in Mesoamerica, however, is not simply of a great number of archetypal features of this kind duplicating features known from Eurasia, but of a distinctive constellation of such features: seasonal festival calendars based on mathematically registered astronomical observations, marking cycles upon cycles of solar, lunar, and planetary periods; a magnificent serpent deity, the Feathered Serpent (Mayan Kukulcan; Nahuatl Quetzalcoatl), incarnated as a god-man and king, who dies and is resurrected; temple towers suggesting Mesopotamian ziggurats; religious images, incense, music, and hieratical processions; and so on and on. It perhaps is merely coincidental that whereas the basal starting date of the Mayan ceremonial calendar is 3113 B.C.,[35] in India the beginning of the present "Great Cycle" *(Mahāyuga)* of 4,320,000 years is supposed to have occurred on February 18, 3102 B.C.[36] Independent observation of the same celestial phenomena as those recognized in Mesopotamia centuries before might well have inspired almost identical cosmologies, distinguished from each other principally by the fact that the Mayan calendar was controlled by a mathematical system of base 20, intermeshing with a week of thirteen days, whereas the early Sumero-Babylonian calendar was of base 60 with a five-day week.

One can only wonder considering, as I have now been considering for some forty-odd years, the likenesses, both in breadth and in depth, of the two constellations of metaphorical images of the Old World and the New, whether the human psyche can possibly be so thoroughgoingly programmed that these two all but identical constellations might indeed have arisen independently in the separated hemispheres of our planet. Some idea of the astonishing intimacy in detail of the great convergence (if that, indeed, is what it is) may be gained simply by confronting, as though of one and the same mystical heritage, such an example of New World iconography as the Navaho sand painting pictured hereafter (see Figure 15, page 71) and the wisdom-lore of India's Old World yoga: treating the first as of the way of what Ramakrishna called the "lovers of God" (see page 40–41), and the other as of the fearless "knowers."

THE METAPHORICAL JOURNEY

In the Navaho sand painting the bounded area is equivalent to the interior of a temple, an Earthly Paradise, where all forms are to be experienced, not in terms of practical relationships, threatening or desirable, evil or good, but as the manifestations of powers supporting the visible world and which, though not recognized in practical living, are everywhere immediately at hand and of one's own nature. The painting is used in a blessing ceremony, for healing, or to impart the courage and spiritual strength requisite to the endurance of some ordeal, or for the performance of some difficult task. The dry painting is of colored sand strewn (with amazing skill and speed) upon the dirt floor of a native dwelling, or hogan. Neighbors and friends have assembled, and for a period of one to five (in many other rituals, nine) continuous nights and days of chanting, prayer, and metaphorical acts, the patient or initiate is ceremonially identified in mind and heart and costume with the mythological protagonist of the relevant legend. He or she actually enters physically into the painting, not simply as the person whose friends and neighbors have solicitously assembled, but equally as a mythic figure engaged in an archetypal adventure of which everyone present knows the design. For it is the archetypal adventure of them all in the knowledge of their individual lives as grounded and participative in a beloved and everlasting pattern. Moreover, all the characters represented in the ceremonial are to be of the local landscape and experience, and become mythologized, so that through a shared witnessing of the ceremonial the entire company is renewed in accord with the nature and beauty of their spiritually instructive world.

The conformity of the imagery of this particular sand painting to the sense and symbolized experiences of the yogic *sushumnā* is certainly astonishing, but not more so than many other concordancies in the myths and ritual arts of peoples across the world. The axial Great Corn Plant corresponds here to the *sushumnā;* the footprints represent a spiritual ascent along the mystic way known to the Navaho as the Pollen Path. There is a verse from a sacred chant:

> In the house of life I wander
> On the pollen path,
> With a god of cloud I wander
> To a holy place.
> With a god ahead I wander
> And a god behind.
> In the house of life I wander
> On the pollen path. [37]

The Great Corn Plant's upper half is marked by a lightning flash, which immediately suggests the oriental *vajra* ("thunderbolt of enlightenment") of Hindu and Buddhist iconography. It strikes to the exact center of the way, which corresponds (if we count the leaf-marked stages, the tassel above, and the root below) exactly to the fourth *cakra, anāhata,* where the sound is heard that is not made by any two things striking together (see page 36). In Navaho myths and legends the god known as Sun Bearer, Tsóhanoai, possesses lightning-arrows. His domicile is above, in the sky, and when his twin sons, conceived of him by an earthly virgin, Changing Woman, arrived to receive from him the power and weapons with which to rid the world of monsters, the solar power of which they then became possessed was so great that when they returned to earth it had to be modified by a deity known as Hastyéyalti (Talking God), maternal grandfather of the pantheon, in whom male and female powers are combined. [38] In the sand painting, the realm of operation of this second god is represented by a modified rainbow of two colors, red and blue (brick red and blue gray in the color reproduction), symbolic respectively of solar energy and of water and the moon. The high place onto which the Twins descended from the heavenly house of their father to earth was the central mountain of the world (locally, Mt. Taylor in New Mexico; height, 11,302 feet) and the corresponding station in the painting is at *cakra* 4, *anāhata.* Moreover, the root of the corn plant is threefold, like *Yuktatriveṇī* in the *mūlādhāra* (see pages 43, 50). The pollen path commences lower right and is of two colors, like the modified rainbow (or like the moon, which is of both matter and light). But at the turn between the Spirit Bringers the path becomes yellow and single (like the fire of the blended breaths, exploding to ascend the *sushumnā;* see pages 44–45); after which, in a sacred way, to an accompaniment of chants and prayer, the sanctuary is entered.

The parallelism of the tantric visionary ascent of the *sushumnā* and the ritually controlled transit of the Navaho Pollen Path is not simple to explain. We know that in Tibetan tantric colleges such as Gyudto in Lhasa, a strictly controlled tradition of ritualized sand painting was practiced until the calamity of 1959. We know also that the Navaho are a people of Athapascan stock, from northwesternmost North America, who migrated to the Southwest some time around the twelfth century A.D. The Athapascans of the Canadian Northwest, however, do not practice sand painting. The Navaho seem to have acquired the art from the Pueblo tribes around whose villages they settled. Any relationship between the Pueblos of New Mexico and the great monasteries of Lhasa is impossible, not only to document, but even to imagine. We are thrown back, therefore, for the present at least, upon the academically unpopular *psychological* explanation of the undeniable parallelism of these two visionary journeys, one, of an ecstatic, immediately visionary kind, the other, by way of a tribal ceremonial.

That the experience of an ascent of the *sushumnā* is of a psychological order is hardly questionable. And that the visions are culturally conditioned (as are all visions and all dreams) is certain; for every petal of the envisioned lotuses, from the four petals of the *mūlādhāra* to the two of *ājñā* and thousand of *sahasrāra*, bears a letter of the Sanskrit alphabet. Yet descriptions of the lotuses by those who have experienced them carry the conviction of a reality, not indeed of a gross material *(sthūla),* but of a subtle *(sukshma),* dreamlike, visionary kind.

"They are formed of Consciousness," said Ramakrishna, "like a tree made of wax—the branches, twigs, fruits, and so forth all of wax." [39] "One cannot see them with the physical eyes. One cannot take them out by cutting open the body." [40]

"Just before my attaining this state of mind," he told his company of followers, "it had been revealed to me how the *kundalini* is aroused, how the lotuses of the different centers blossom forth, and how all this culminates in *samādhi.* This is a very secret experience. I saw a boy twenty-two or twenty-three years old, exactly resembling me, enter the *sushumnā* nerve and commune with the lotuses, touching them with his tongue. He began with the center at the anus and passed through the centers at the sexual organ, navel, and so on. The different lotuses of those centers—four-petalled, six-petalled, ten-petalled, and so forth—had been drooping. At his touch they stood erect.

"When he reached the heart—I distinctly remember it—and communed with the lotus there, touching it with his tongue, the twelve-petalled lotus, which was hanging head down, stood erect and opened its petals. Then he came to the sixteen-petalled lotus in the throat and the two-petalled lotus in the forehead. And last of all, the thousand-petalled lotus in the head blossomed. Since then I have been in this state." [41]

In the sand painting of the Pollen Path, the two colors of the "female" and the "male," lunar and solar powers, having become one on passing between the guardian Spirit Bringers at the entrance to the sanctuary; the path, which is now of the single color of pollen, runs to the base of the World Tree, where three roots or ways of entrance are confronted. Those to right and to left point separately to the separated Spirit Bringers, whose arms and hands gesture together toward the portal of the middle way. The lower half, then, of the axial corn plant, which is to represent the graded stages of an initiation, is found signalized by a rainbow of the same two colors that were already of the initiate's pollen path of virtue before its right turn to the Spirit Bringer's call.

Now a rainbow is an insubstantial apparition composed of both matter and light, formed opposite the sun by reflection and refraction of the sun's rays in drops of rain. Thus it is at once material and immaterial, lunar and solar, as the matched colors, blue and red, here suggest. One thinks of the words of Goethe's Faust at the end of the opening scene of *Faust,* Part II, where, bedded on a flowery turf, Faust wakes to an alpine sunrise and beholds across the valley a rainbow spread across the face of a mighty waterfall. The sun behind him being too powerful to contemplate directly, his eyes dwell, "with rapture ever growing," upon the beauty of the insubstantial image formed of the sun's light refracted in the whirling spray of the tumbling torrent, and he exclaims, *"So bleibe denn die Sonne mir im Rücken* ['So let the sun remain then behind me!']....*Am farbigen Abglanz haben wir das Leben* ['Our living is in the colorful reflection']." For he is stationed at the crucial turning point of *cakra* 4, *anāhata;* there he must choose whether to pass, like an Indian yogi, to extinction in the full blast of the sun or to rest engaged in the field of action, held to the recognition of the play of the sun's light through all the forms given life by its power!

The rainbow of the sand painting ends exactly midway of the path. There the lightning strikes, and to right and to left two apparitions appear. These are of a spiritual messenger-fly known to the Navaho as Dontso, "Big Fly," and in his second aspect, "Little Wind." In art and myth this little figure holds a prominent place, and like everything else in Navaho mythology, he is a transformation into metaphor of an actual feature of the environment. There is, namely, a local tachinid fly, of the species *Hystricia pollinosa van der Wulp,* which has the habit of lighting on a person's shoulder or on the chest just in front of the shoulder.[42] In this role it has been admitted to the pantheon as a bringer of news and guidance and as a messenger of the spirit. In its present, dual apparition, black and pale yellow, it represents separately the male and female energies, which in the rainbow are united. For both black and red, in the color system of this painting, are symbolic of male energy, while both yellow and blue are female. Black is sinister and threatening to life, yet also protects. The lightning flash here is black, and Black Wind (which here appears in the form of the black Dontso) is the power of the sun.[43] Yellow represents, in contrast, fructification, pollen, and the powers of vegetation. Women originated from a yellow corn ear, and yellow is the color of an inexhaustible food bowl symbolizing sustenance.[44] The black zigzag line of the lightning flash is single, whereas in the rainbow, where the male power has been tempered to the female power, the male is red and the female blue. Red is the color of danger, war, and sorcery, but also of their safeguards; for it is the color, as well, of blood, flesh, and nourishing meat.[45] Blue is a color associated by the Navaho with the fructifying power of the earth, with water and with sky.[46] Combined as here in a rainbow, the two are known as "The Sunray" and said to stand for "light rays emerging from a cloud when the sun is behind it..."[47]

The cornstalk of this painting is blue, and upon the central corn tassel at its top there is a bird, also blue, symbolic, it is said, of dawn, happiness, and promise. [48] The only two ears of corn to be seen are at nodes corresponding (by analogy with *sushumnā*) to *cakras* 3 and 4, *maṇipūra* and *anāhata*, both of which are associated with powers and realizations of the period, in a lifetime, of maturity—mastery and illumination—which may or may not be by coincidence.

For the artist to whom we owe the reproduction of this precious document of an orally communicated tradition that is rapidly disappearing did not receive an interpretation of its symbols from the Singer (the Medicine Man) from whose Blessing Rite it was drawn. We now have, however, an ample resource of well-collected materials authoritatively interpreted, assembled by scholars chiefly of the 1930s and 1940s (when the normal Navaho household was said to have comprised a father and mother, one child and two anthropologists), out of whose publications a substantially acceptable reading of such an iconographic work can be confidently reconstructed.

My own researches in the material were undertaken in those same years of the 1930s and 1940s in connection, partly, with my task of editing, for the opening of the Bollingen Series, Maud Oakes's collection of paintings from the war ceremonial of the old Navaho warrior and medicine man Jeff King (1852/60(?)–1964, now buried with honors in Arlington National Cemetery), *Where the Two Came to Their Father*, published in 1943. [49] At the same time I was at work with Henry Morton Robinson on *A Skeleton Key to Finnegans Wake* (1944), besides helping Swami Nikhilananda with his translation from Bengali of *The Gospel of Sri Ramakrishna* (1942), having just commenced the twelve-year task of editing for the Bollingen Series four publications from the posthumous papers of my deceased friend Heinrich Zimmer: *Myths and Symbols in Indian Art and Civilization* (Bollingen Series VI, 1946), *The King and the Corpse* (Bollingen Series XI, 1948), *Philosophies of India* (Bollingen Series XXVI, 1951), and *The Art of Indian Asia*, in two volumes (Bollingen Series XXXIX, 1955).

My distinct impression throughout those years was that I was at work only on separate chapters of a single mythological epic of the human imagination. Moreover, the epic was the same as that to which I had been introduced twenty years before in my graduate studies at Columbia University in anthropology and European romantic and medieval literatures; in Paris at the Sorbonne on the Provençal poets and Arthurian romance; and at the University of Munich in Sanskrit and Far Eastern Buddhist art. Adolf Bastian's theory of a concord throughout the mythologies of the world of certain *Elementargedanken,* "elementary ideas" *(Das Beständige in den Menschenrassen,* Berlin, 1868), was confirmed for me beyond question by these apparently far-flung researches. The first task of any systematic comparison of the myths and religions of mankind should therefore be (it seemed to me) to identify these universals (or, as C. G. Jung termed them, archetypes of the unconscious) and as far as possible to interpret them; and the second task then should be to recognize and interpret the various locally and historically conditioned transformations of the metaphorical images through which these universals have been rendered.

Since the archetypes, or elementary ideas, are not limited in their distributions by cultural or even linguistic boundaries, they cannot be defined as culturally determined. However, the local metaphors by which they have been everywhere connoted, the local ways of experiencing and applying their force, are indeed socially conditioned and defined. Bastian termed such local figurations "ethnic ideas," *Völkergedanken,* and Mircea Eliade has termed them "hierophanies" (from *hieros-,* "powerful, supernatural, holy, sacred," plus *phainein,* "to reveal, show, make known").

"The very dialectic of the sacred," Eliade declares, "tends to repeat a series of archetypes, so that a hierophany realized at a certain historical moment is structurally equivalent to a hierophany a thousand years earlier or later." Furthermore, "hierophanies have the peculiarity of seeking to reveal the sacred in its totality, even if the human beings in whose consciousness the sacred 'shows itself' fasten upon only one aspect or one small part of it. In the most elementary hierophany *everything is declared.* The manifestation of the sacred in a stone or a tree is neither less mysterious nor less noble than its manifestation as a 'god.' The process of sacralizing reality is the same; the *forms* taken by the process in man's religious consciousness differ." [50]

The elementary idea is grounded in the psyche; the ethnic idea through which it is rendered, in local geography, history, and society. A hierophany occurs when through some detail, whether of a local landscape, artifact, social custom, historical memory, or individual biography, a psychological archetype or elementary idea is reflected. The object so informed becomes thereby sacralized, or mythologized. Correspondingly, a religious *experience* will be realized when there is felt an immediate sense of *identification* with the revelation. The sense of a mere *relationship* is not the same. In popular cult the experience of relationship is frequently all that is intended. Thereby a sense of social solidarity may be rendered. Through identification, however, a transformation of character is effected.

METAPHORICAL IDENTIFICATION

In the Blessing Ceremony of the Navaho the psychosomatic healing of spiritual initiation is accomplished by means of an identification, ritually induced, of the patient or initiate with the mythological adventure of the Pollen Path in its threshold crossings into and through a sacred space and out into the world transformed. We have not been told by what specific prayers, chants, and metaphorical acts the adventure is conducted. The pictorial statement of the painting, however, indicates the transformative stages.

Footprints of white cornmeal mark the path of the initiate throughout. As already noticed, they approach along a road that is of the two symbolic colors of the male and female powers, fire and water, sunlight and cloud, which at the place of the Spirit Bringers abruptly blend to one golden yellow of the color of pollen. The same color of pollen then appears bordering the outspread sacred space, which in this way opens to a display of the indwelling powers of pollen.

There are no footprints on this part of the path. To be assumed is a threshold passage of the mind as it turns from secular anxieties, identifications, and expectations, to a game of make believe ("as if"; *als ob*, recalling Kant; see pages 29–30), assuming an intentionally metaphorical, mythological cast of hierophantic personifications. The Navaho have a number of procedures to effect this indispensable alteration of consciousness: sweat baths, solemn recitations of the names of the gods to be represented in the

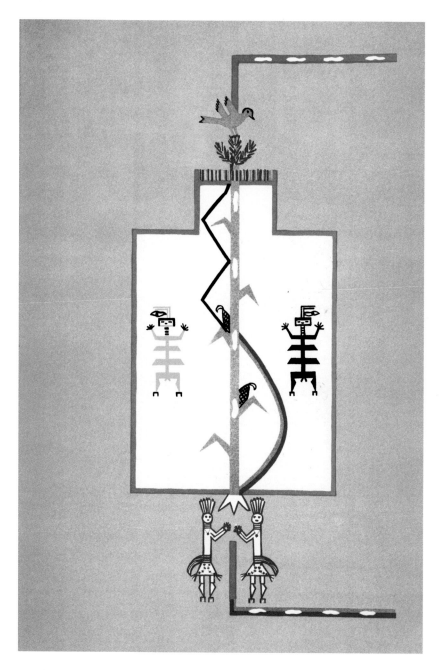

Figure 15. Navaho sand painting to a Blessing Chant. New Mexico, c. 1950.

rite, heraldic face and body painting, with an investiture of ornaments such as the god with whom the candidate is to identify would be wearing. The ordeal is an act of sacrifice. The mind is to abandon forever the whole way of relating to life that is of the knowledge of the two powers of the path only as distinct from each other, red and blue. Beyond the exit gate, returning to the world, the path is to be no longer red and blue, but of the one color of pollen. The neighbors and friends who have gathered to witness the occasion will experience an exaltation, but then return to the world along the path by which they came; for their participation will have been, not of identification, but of a relationship—something comparable to the attendance by a Roman Catholic family at Holy Mass, whereas the initiate, nearly naked and decorated as a god, will have become identified with the adventure, as in the way of the words of Jesus reported in the Thomas Gospel: "Whoever drinks from My mouth shall become as I am and I myself will become he, and the hidden things shall be revealed to him" (Logion 109).[51]

When footprints reappear in the painting they are already in or on the cornstalk, and Dontso has appeared as at once female and male, yellow and black, in two aspects: the one as two and the two as one. Moreover, the path of blue and red is now beheld in the luminous form of the Sunray, no longer of solid matter, but of light and cloud.

In the Hindu ascent of the *sushumnā,* the *cakras* of the lower centers are identified, respectively, as of the elements Earth, Water, and Fire, the associated divinities being Brahmā the Creator, Viṣṇu as Preserver and Lover, and Śiva as the Destroyer of Obstructions to Illumination. The involved yogi becomes to such a degree absorbed in these morphogenetic archetypes that as the *kuṇḍalinī* ascends, the whole body below the center of concentration goes cold. As stated by Sir John Woodroffe: "There is one simple test whether the Śakti [the energy as *kuṇḍalinī*] is actually aroused. When she is aroused intense heat is felt at that spot, but when she leaves a particular center the part so left becomes as cold and apparently lifeless as a corpse. The progress upwards may thus be externally verified by others. When the Śakti (Power) has reached the upper brain *(sahasrāra)* the whole body is cold and corpse-like; except the top of the skull, where some warmth is felt, this being the place where the static and kinetic aspects of Consciousness unite."[52]

Kuṇḍalinī yoga practiced in this outright way, in other words, is not a game of "as if" and make-believe, but an actual experience of psychological absorption in a metaphysical ground of some kind, a morphogenetic field that has not yet, as far as I know, been scientifically recognized in the West except by C. G. Jung and, lately, by the physicist Rupert Sheldrake, whose works, according to one concerned scientific reviewer, ought to be burned. Ramakrishna, who surely knew whereof he spoke, warned (as we have already learned), that not only is this form of yoga extremely difficult, but also should not be practiced by the lovers of God, since (in his words): "To one who follows it even the divine play in the world becomes like a dream and appears unreal; his 'I' also vanishes."[53] At *cakra 4, anāhata,* where the sound OM is first heard that is not made by any two things striking together, the element into which the yogi is absorbed is Air *(vāyu,* the life-breath; *prāṇa, spiritus,* pure spirit); while at *cakra 5* he devolves into *ākāsa,* Space. "Boundless am I as Space!" exclaims the ancient sage, Aṣṭāvakra. "The phenomenal world is like an empty jar [enclosing Space, which nevertheless is boundless]. Thus known, phenomenality need be neither renounced, accepted, nor destroyed."[54]

In Dante's *Divina Commedia* the corresponding stage of spiritual exaltation extends through all but the last three cantos of the *Paradiso* (I–XXX), telling of the visionary's ecstatic ascent, led by the spirit of Beatrice (Dante's Śakti), from the garden of the Earthly Paradise on the summit of Mount Purgatory, through all the ranges of space to the outermost sphere of the Primum Mobile, by which the heavens are revolved.

> A Light is thereabove which makes the Creator
>   visible to every creature that has
>   his peace only in beholding Him.
> It spreads so wide a circle that the
>   circumference would be too large
>   a girdle for the sun.
> Its whole expanse is made by a ray reflected
>   from the summit of the Primum
>   Mobile, which therefrom takes its life and potency.[55]

The comparable figure in the Indian system is of the *nāda,* the creative sound OM of the energy of the light, ever resounding in the *ākāsa:* beyond which "space," both in Dante's concluding cantos *(Paradiso* XXXI–XXXIII) and in the stations six and seven of the Indian *sushumnā,* the culminating experiences are, first, of the vision of one's image of God and, then, of a transcendent Light which is the energy of the living world.

In oriental art, the image, whether of the Buddha, of Brahmā, of Viṣṇu, or of Śiva, is normally shown seated or standing upon a lotus. In Dante's vision, the Trinity with the whole heavenly host is beheld within the corolla of a radiant, pure white rose.[56] In the Navaho sand painting the final image above and beyond the enclosed white space of the pollen-framed ceremonial field is of a symbolic bird perched on the central tassel at the top of the sacred corn plant. Noticing that the tassels are three, as are also the roots of the plant in the earth below, one is reminded that in Dante's *Divina Commedia* his vision of a Trinity above is matched by his Satan in the bowels of the earth (see page 49), whose head shows three faces: the left face black, the right between white and yellow, and the middle red, signifying, respectively, in Dante's intention, ignorance, hatred, and impotent rage, in express contrast to the wisdom, love, and omnipotence of the Godhead.[57]

In the Old Norse image of the World Ash, Yggdrasil, upon which Othin hung himself for nine days and nights in a sacrifice of himself to Himself to gain the wisdom of the runes (the scripture of the gods),[58] there is an eagle perched on the topmost branch, and beneath, a dragon gnawing at the roots, of which there are three.[59] The bird is a universal symbol of the spirit and spiritual flight, as is the feather of spiritual power. In India the wild gander, *haṃsa,* is symbolic of the *ātman,* the Self, and such a perfected saint as Ramakrishna is known as a Paramahaṃsa, ("Paramount or Supreme Wild Gander"). Jesus at the moment of his baptism saw a dove descending from the heavens. Zeus approached Leda in the aspect of a swan. Serpents and dragons, in contrast, are of the earth, its dynamism, urges, and demonic wisdom.

"The Pharisees and the Scribes have received the keys of Knowledge," said the Gnostic Jesus to St. Thomas and the disciples, "they have hidden them. They did not enter, and they did not let those enter who wished. But you, become wise as serpents and innocent as doves" (Logion 39).[60]

For the two modes of consciousness are of the one life, whereas the cherubim and flaming sword have forbidden entrance, even of the "justified," to the earthly garden where the two become again one.

Accordingly, in Dante's vision, Heaven and Hell are still separate, and the lower power (ethically judged) has been eternally condemned. The descent of the spirit is a fall. The life-giving demon has become a devil. The axial tree of the universe, around which all revolves, that is to say, is still cut in two, as it was in Yahweh's Eden of the two trees, one, of the Knowledge of Good and Evil, and the other, of the Knowledge of Eternal Life. Whereas in the unreformed, primeval archetype of the World Tree, such as appears in the Old Norse Yggdrasil and in the Navaho Blue Corn Stalk, the life-giving roots and the pollen-bearing flowerings, or tassels, are of a single, organically intact, mythological image.

In the metaphorical Promised Land or Earthly Paradise of the Navaho sand painting *(paradise,* from the Greek *paradeisos,* "enclosed park"; Old Persian *pairi,* "around," and *daēza,* "wall," giving *pairidaēza,* "enclosure"), the rainbow curve, springing red and blue from the root, covers the zone of the first three *cakras* to the node of the second fruiting, where lightning strikes, flashing from the summit. The white footprints of the ceremonial path do not identify the initiate with either the rainbow or the lightning, only with the middle way; which is to say, apparently, that there is to be no absorption of the individual in identifications either with the gross matter of the world or with the unembodied light of sheer spirit. Both are recognized, evidently, as attributes of the Pollen Path. But the ordeal is to hold to the way between; so that even on coming to and passing the station of the Bluebird (Paramahaṁsa), the path, now the color of pollen (which is the color by which the garden is enclosed), does not ascend to the sky, but turning abruptly again to the right, bears the footprints back to the dwelling from which they came.

THE NET OF GEMS

The yogi experiencing nondual identification of the Self *(ātman)* with the Being, Consciousness, and Bliss which transcends yet moves the universe and all beings *(sac-cid-ānanda brahman),* may remain so fixed in this rapture of *cakras* 6 and 7 ("realized disengagement, perfected isolation, absolute unification," *kaivalyam)* that his body is abandoned, to continue as a dried leaf blown by a wind until it goes to pieces. Such, they say, is the spiritual state of the wandering mendicant, *sannyāsin.* As described by

Shankara: "Though doing, he is inactive, though bearing the fruits of past acts, unaware of them; disembodied though embodied, omnipresent though locally walking about: such a knower of *brahman,* everywhere living on as though bodiless, is ever untouched by either pleasure or pain, goodness or evil."[61]

Or the one thus "released while living" *(jīvanmukta)* may voluntarily return to the state of mind of *cakra* 4, either in the way of a Mahāyāna Bodhisattva whose "being" *(sattva)* is "illumination" *(bodhi),* touched by compassion for all suffering beings, who, renouncing for himself release from rebirth, returns to the world as a teaching savior (see again Philippians 2:6–8); or in the way simply of one fulfilled in the knowledge of an eternal mystery at play through himself as through all the productions of time, and who is thus competent to participate with joy and courage, in the sorrows of the world. As interpreted by Arthur Avalon (Sir John Woodroffe):

> If the ultimate Reality is one which exists in two aspects, of quiescent enjoyment of the Self in Liberation from all form and of active enjoyment of objects—that is, as pure "Spirit" and [as] "Spirit" in matter—then a complete union with Reality demands such unity in both of its aspects. It must be known both "here" *(Iha)* and "there" *(Amutra)*. . . . It is the one Śiva who is the supreme blissful experience, and who appears in the form of man with a life of mingled pleasure and pain. Both happiness here and the bliss of liberation here and hereafter may be attained if the identity of these Śivas be realized in every human act. This will be achieved by making every human function, without exception, a religious act of sacrifice and worship *(Yajna)*. . . . And so the Tantrik *Sādhaka* (adept), when eating or drinking, or fulfilling any of the other natural functions of the body, does so, saying and believing, *Śivo'ham* ("I am Śiva"), *Bhairavo'ham* ("I am Bhairava"), *Sā'ham* ("I am She"). It is not merely the separate individual who thus acts and enjoys. It is Śiva who does so *in* and *through* him.[62]

In the words of the legendary Aṣṭāvakra: "Having realized the Self in all and all in the Self, released from egoism and the sense of 'mine' be happy *(sukhi bhava,* 'enjoy')!"[63]

By comparison with these yogic realizations the initiations rendered through the Navaho sand paintings may be likened to that of *cakra* 4, where the sounding is heard of the syllable OM through all of nature. In *The Indians' Book* (1907), Natalie Curtis wrote of her attendance at a healing ceremony.

> To the white man there is scarcely a more impressive sight than a group of Navahos chanting these ancient traditional songs, which have been learned and handed down with the greatest accuracy and care. The quiet, monotonous quality of the chant seems heightened by the concentration of the singers, who, with closed eyes or fixed gaze, bend every thought upon their singing that they may not err in word or sequence of the holy song.
>
> At a healing-ceremony in some hogan where there is sickness, the steady rhythm of the medicine-songs pulses all night long, groups of singers on opposite sides of the fire vying with one another in endurance. Does one group flag, another starts in freshly, and so, like the central pile of burning logs, the song flares unextinguished till the paling of the stars. Then comes a pause—the song changes; all the voices join in chanting, and then in measured cadence rises a *Hozhonji* song [a "Mountain Song"] to end the ceremony of the night and greet the coming day. The singing of a *Hozhonji* song is at all times an act of consecration. [64]
>
> These songs describe a journey to a holy place beyond the sacred mountains where are everlasting life and blessedness. The Divine Ones who live in and beyond the mountains made the songs, and so they tell of a journey as a home-coming.
>
> When these songs are sung over a man, the spirit of the man makes the journey that the song describes. Upon the rainbow he moves from mountain to mountain, for it is thus that the gods travel, standing upon the rainbow. The rainbow is swift as lightning. [65]
>
> > Swift and far I journey,
> > Swift upon the rainbow.
> > Swift and far I journey,
> > Lo, yonder, the Holy Place!
> > > Yea, swift and far I journey.

To Sisnajinni, and beyond it,
    Yea, swift and far I journey;
The Chief of Mountains, and beyond it,
    Yea, swift and far I journey;
To Life Unending, and beyond it,
    Yea, swift and far I journey;
To Joy Unchanging, and beyond it,
    Yea, swift and far I journey.

Homeward now shall I journey,
Homeward upon the rainbow;
    [etc.]

Homeward behold me starting,
Homeward upon the rainbow;
    [etc.]

Homeward behold me faring,
Homeward upon the rainbow;
    [etc.]

Now arrived home behold me
Now arrived on the rainbow;
Now arrived home behold me,
Lo, here, the Holy Place!

Yea, now arrived home behold me,
At Sisnajinni, and beyond it,
    Yea, now arrived home behold me;
The Chief of Mountains, and beyond it,
    Yea, now arrived home behold me;
In Life Unending, and beyond it,
    Yea, now arrived home behold me;
In Joy Unchanging, and beyond it,
    Yea, now arrived home behold me.

Seated at home behold me,
Seated amid the rainbow,

Seated at home behold me,
Lo, here, the Holy Place!

Yea, seated at home behold me.
At Sisnajinni and beyond it,
    Yea, seated at home behold me;
The Chief of Mountains, and beyond it,
    Yea, seated at home behold me;
In Life Unending, and beyond it,
    Yea, seated at home behold me;
In Joy Unchanging, and beyond it,
    Yea, seated at home behold me. [66]

"The *Hozhonji* songs," say the Navaho, "are holy songs, given to us by the gods." [67]

Whatever the reality may be—the being or nonbeing—of the mysterious morphogenetic field into which the enraptured yogi lets dissolve his humanity and its world, detailed comparative studies of the tantric iconographies associated with those raptures and the greatly various yet morphologically homologous initiation rites and mythologies of revelation that have been observed and recorded from every part of the planet, make it evident that the yogi is losing himself in exactly those psychological (and therefore biologically grounded) universals—Adolf Bastian's "elementary ideas," C. G. Jung's "archetypes of the unconscious"—which have been forever the connoted field of reference of the metaphors of myth. The burnt-out, wandering *sannyāsin* has followed the connotations to the end. Fulfilled gurus, seers, incarnations, and saviors, speak frequently as with one voice.

Said the Gnostic Jesus: "If those who lead you say to you: 'See, the Kingdom is in heaven,' then the birds of the heaven will precede you. If they say to you: 'It is in the sea,' then the fish will precede you. But the Kingdom is within you and it is without you. If you will know yourselves, then you will be known and you will know that you are the sons of the Living Father. But if you do not know yourselves, then you are in poverty and you are poverty" (Logion 3). [68] "I am the Light that is above them all, I am the All, the All came forth from Me and the All attained to Me"

(Logion 77).[69] "Whoever drinks from My mouth shall become as I am and I myself will become he, and the hidden things shall be revealed to him" (Logion 108).[70]

"I am the universal *ātman,* I am the All!" exclaims the illuminated disciple of the great guru of gurus, Shankara. "I am transcendent, non-dual, unrelated, infinite knowledge. Sheer bliss am I, indivisible."[71] And from the master Aṣṭāvakra: "You pervade the universe and the universe exists in you. You are by nature Pure Consciousness. Do not be small-minded!"[72]

The universally distinguishing characteristic of mythological thought and communication is an implicit connotation through all its metaphorical imagery of a sense of identity of some kind, transcendent of appearances, which unites behind the scenes the opposed actors on the world stage. Schopenhauer, in his bold and really magnificent "Transcendent Speculation upon an Apparent Intention in the Fate of the Individual" (1850),[73] takes up the idea, remarking that in the later years of a lifetime, looking back over the course of one's days and noticing how encounters and events that appeared at the time to be accidental became the crucial structuring features of an unintended life story through which the potentialities of one's character were fostered to fulfillment, one may find it difficult to resist the notion of the course of one's biography as comparable to that of a cleverly constructed novel, wondering who the author of the surprising plot can have been; considering further, that as the shaping of one's own life was largely an effect of personalities accidentally encountered, so, too, one must oneself have worked effects upon others. The whole context of world history, in fact, is of destinies unfolding through time as a vast net of reciprocal influences of this kind, which not only are of people upon people, but involve also the natural world with its creatures and accidents of all kinds. Invoking the analogy of dream, the philosopher reminds his reader that in dream the unanticipated occurrences, which appear to be accidental and occasionally, as in nightmare, terrifying, are actually of a context composed and controlled according to an unsuspected intention which is of none other than one's own will, "put forward from a standpoint, however, that is not of the dreaming consciousness."[74] Comparably, the dream or nightmare of our lives is a production of our own hidden will. But the dreams and lives of all interlock, as though of a single, superordinated context; "so that," as the philosopher observes, "in the way of a veritable *Harmonia praestabiliter,* each dreams only to accord with his own metaphysical associations, yet all the life-dreams are interlocked so artfully that each, though experiencing only what is profitable to himself, is yet fulfilling the requirements of others. . . .

"Our hesitation before such a colossal thought will perhaps be diminished by the recollection," Schopenhauer suggests in conclusion, "that the ultimate dreamer of the vast life-dream is finally, in a certain sense, but one, namely the Will to Live, and that the multiplicity of appearances follows from the conditioning effects of time and space [the morphogenetic field whereby the Will to Live assumes forms]. It is one great dream dreamed by a single Being, but in such a way that all the dream characters dream too. Hence, everything links and accords with everything else."[75]

The Indian image of the "Net of Gems," where in every gem of the net all the others are reflected, is a counterpart of this idea. Another likeness may be seen in the Buddhist doctrine of "mutual arising" *(pratītya-samutpāda),* as represented in the Mahāyāna "Flower Wreath Sūtra," the *Avata-ṃsaka* (Japanese, *Kegon),* which has been defined as a theory of the "causation of the universe and its events by the common action-influence of all beings."[76] Another image is of the Hindu divinity Viṣṇu couched on the back of the Cosmic Serpent, Ananta ("Unending"), floating on the Cosmic Milky Ocean, dreaming the dream of the Universe—to which image and universal dream James Joyce in *Finnegans Wake* correlated, with an Irish twist, the whole spectacle of world history.

Schopenhauer was apparently the first philosopher to realize that Immanuel Kant in *The Critique of Pure Reason* (1781) not only had demolished the philosophical mansions both of Cartesian rationalism (the French eighteenth-century Enlightenment) and of Baconian empiricism (Anglo-Saxon "common sense"), but also had established the prerequisites for a correlation of oriental and occidental metaphysical terms. For Kant's *a priori* forms of sensibility (time and space) and *a priori* categories of judgment—(1) of *quantity:* unity, plurality, and universality; (2) of *quality:* affirmation, negation, and limitation; (3) of *relation:* substantiality, causation, and reciprocity; and (4) of *modality:* possibility, actuality, and necessity—are exactly India's *māyā* (from the verbal root *mā,* "to form, to build"), that deluding faculty of mind by which *brahman-ātman* (= Kant's "Thing-in-itself") is veiled from direct experience and projected transformed as the phenomena of space-time.

Schopenhauer's own crucial contribution, then, was in his realization that whereas our outer eyes do indeed behold only phenomenal appearances *(Vorstellungen)* within a three-dimensional field of space-time *(Die Welt als Vorstellung)*, the inward experience of each and every one of those appearances is of him-, her-, or itself as a willing subject *(Die Welt als Wille)*, this inward experience of the Will to Live then being, in fact, a veiled experience within oneself of the energy of *ātman-brahman,* the universal Self, as linked however to *saṃsāra* (the temporal, apparitional field) by the apparition's own fear of death and desire for continued apparitional existence. The impulse of one's Will to Life, that is to say, is the inward experience of the *ātman* as oneself; and the correlative outward experience of the *ātman* as another occurs—as Schopenhauer recognized—*only* by way of the insight of "compassion" *(karuṇā),* which is the quality of a Bodhisattva.

"How is it possible," he asks in his celebrated essay *On the Foundation of Morality,* "How is it possible that suffering that is neither my own nor of my concern should immediately affect me as though it were my own, and with such force that it moves me to action? . . . This is something really mysterious, something for which Reason can provide no explanation, and for which no basis can be found in practical experience. It is nevertheless of common occurrence, and everyone has had the experience. It is not unknown even to the most hard-hearted and self-interested. Examples appear every day before our eyes of instant responses of the kind, without reflection, one person helping another, coming to his aid, even setting his own life in clear danger for someone whom he has seen for the first time, having nothing more in mind than that the other is in need and in peril of his life. . . . "[77]

Schopenhauer's answer to his question is that this immediate reaction and response represents the breakthrough of a *metaphysical* realization—namely (as he states the idea in Sanskrit), *"tat tvam asi,* thou art that."[78]

"This presupposes," he declares, "that I have to some extent identified myself with the other and therewith removed for the moment the barrier between the 'I' and the 'Not-I'. Only then can the other's situation, his want, his need, become mine. I then no longer see him in the way of an empirical perception, as one strange to me, indifferent to me, completely other than myself; but in him I suffer, in spite of the fact that his skin does not enfold my nerves...."79

"Individuation is but an appearance in a field of space and time, these being the conditioning forms through which my cognitive faculties apprehend their objects. Hence the multiplicity and differences that distinguish individuals are likewise but appearances. They exist, that is to say, only in my mental representation *(in meiner Vorstellung)*. My own true inner being actually exists in every living creature as truly and immediately as known to my consciousness only in myself. This realization, for which the standard formula in Sanskrit is *tat tvam asi,* is the ground of that compassion *(Mitleid)* upon which all true, that is to say unselfish, virtue rests and whose expression is in every good deed."80

The metaphors of any mythology may be defined as affect signs derived from intuitions of just this play of the Self through all the forms of a local manner of life, made manifest through ritualized representations, pedagogical narratives, prayers, meditations, annual festivals, and the like, in such a way that all members of the relevant community may be held, both in mind and in sentiment, to its knowledge and thus moved to live in accord. An atmosphere of dream prevails throughout, since everything is represented, and to be experienced, as the hierophany (to use again Eliade's term) of a mystery that is not of the plane of the manifestations themselves, but transcendent of their issues. "There is a dream dreaming us," declared a Kalahari Bushman to Laurens van der Post. *La vída es sueño* (*Life Is a Dream*) is the title of a play by Calderón. Everything in such a vision of the world-in-being is held and moves in relationship to everything else, to accord with an end that is not of the order of time, yet is everywhere fulfilled in time. William Blake's statement in *The Marriage of Heaven and Hell,* "Eternity is in love with the productions of time," is an adumbration of the paradoxology of the game of hide-and-seek that Nonduality is playing with and in celebration of itself in *la divina commedia* of this night of its dream.

José Ortega y Gasset, in his *Meditaciones del Quijote (Meditations on Don Quixote,* 1914), wrote of the sobering crisis in occidental mentation that occurred at the time of Galileo's invention of the telescope and application of mathematical analysis to an exposition of the mechanical laws governing the universe. At that moment, nature, which formerly had been responsive to the psychological requirements and expectations of mythological heroes, became hard and fast and apart; so that when Don Quixote imagined himself to be riding his nag Rocinante against certain giants that his adventure required, what his lance actually encountered was the revolving sail of a windmill, which overthrew both him and his mount. He saved the adventure for himself, however, by inventing a magician who had transformed the required giants into windmills.

From the standpoint of an exclusively mechanistic view of human experience and action, any such attribution to nature of "a presence...far more deeply interfused" as that of Wordsworth's poetic lines of meditation written above Tintern Abbey, or of Schopenhauer's "Will in Nature," must be qualified in a derogatory sense as the romantic ascription to inanimate nature of human traits and feelings—the so-called pathetic fallacy: a sentimental projection of the imagination like Don Quixote's morbid fantasy of a magician's work in a windmill. Anthropologists, in the same vein, describe as "animism" the attribution in tribal mythologies, not only of consciousness, but also of a discrete indwelling spirit, to every material form of reality, whether it be animal, plant, stone, star, moon, sun, or cyclone. While in the vocabulary of Judeo-Christian theology, diabolism is the word for such beliefs.

For already in the Old Testament, as in the post-Galilean sciences, there is in nature itself no divinity. There is no god in all the earth but in Israel (2 Kings 5:15), and the gods of the Gentiles are devils. The texts of Christian missionaries to this same point in justification of their labors are legion, Satan himself being there recognized as even literally present in the idols, sacraments, sorceries, and miracles of every worship but the mission's own.

Such uninspired literalism in the understanding of mythological metaphors is difficult to match in the whole great field of the history of religions. In popular beliefs there is everywhere, of course, the notion of gods as living entities inhabiting a mythological zone beyond time. But that timeless zone is everywhere conceived to be the ground of the informing spirituality of the visible world itself. In dream and vision one enters into it, and on waking returns. Moreover, as such inward experiences have let us know, its apparitions are of a self-luminous substance revelatory of the vital energies, not only of ourselves but of all living things. The yogi allows his individuated mind to dissolve into the elementary vortices out of which these apparitions appear. In ceremonials such as that of the Navaho Spirit Bringers, their forms have become defined in art as local metaphors connotative of the universal powers they represent. However, the daunting biblical image of the flaming sword between the cherubim, turning every way at the gate of Eden to guard the way to the tree of eternal life, has kept separate the opposed powers of the two guardians, which in the image of the Navaho Pollen Path, no less than in that of the Indian *sushumnā*, must be brought together if the middle way is ever to be opened. In this exceptional tradition, Eternity and Time, Heaven and Earth, are permanently apart. There can be no reading of the images of God and Satan as metaphors of any kind. They are invisible, supernatural facts. And the creatures of this visible earth are but dust, as is the earth itself (Genesis 3:19).

Wherefore, as Blake declares in his own poetic revelation, *The Marriage of Heaven and Hell:*

> The cherub with his flaming sword is hereby commanded to leave his guard at the tree of life, and when he does, the whole creation will be consumed, and appear infinite, and holy, whereas it now appears finite and corrupt.
>
> This will come to pass by an improvement of sensual enjoyment.
>
> But first the notion that man has a body distinct from his soul is to be expunged.
>
> If the doors of perception were cleansed every thing would appear to man as it is, infinite.
>
> For man has closed himself up, till he sees all things thro' the narrow chinks of his cavern.

For modern Western man, that is to say. For in all other parts of the world, in-so-far at least as they have not yet learned of the garden of the two separate trees, *Alles Vergängliche ist nur ein Gleichnis,* "Everything transitory is but a metaphor."[81] But equally, *Alles Unvergängliche ist nur ein Gleichnis,* "Everything eternal is but a metaphor."[82] For as already told, long since, in the Kena Upaniṣad: "That [which is beyond every name and form] is comprehended only by the one with no comprehension of it: anyone comprehending, knows it not. Unknown to the knowing, it is to the unknowing known."[83]

Hence, as the light of the moon (a) is to that of the sun (b), so my mortal life (c) and the lives of all around me (c) are to that *ātman-brahman* (x) which is absolutely beyond name, form, relationship, and definition.

CHAPTER III

The Way of Art

My wife, Jean Erdman, who is a dancer and choreographer, discussing one day the relevance of an appreciation of the psychological connotations of myth to the practice of an art, remarked: "The way of the mystic and the way of the artist are related, except that the mystic doesn't have a craft." The craft holds the artist to the world, whereas the mystic, facing inward, may be carried to such an extreme posture of indifference to the claims of phenomenal life as that of the old yogi with his parasol of grass in the Hindu exemplary tale, "The Humbling of Indra" (pages 24–25).

The king-god of that tale, left sitting on his throne alone when the two humiliating apparitions had vanished like the figments of a dream, had no longer the slightest desire to go on with the construction of his palace. Unsettled forever in his conceit of himself as the governing power of the universe, he summoned his architect, Vishvakarman, thanked him for his engineering feats, heaped on him jewels and precious gifts, and after a sumptuous celebration, sent him home. Desiring nothing now but release from the burden of his inconsequential role, the god entrusted charge of the course of history to his son, and was on the point of retiring to practice yoga in the forest, when his beautiful and passionate queen, Shachī, turned in consternation for comfort and advice to the palace chaplain,

Bṛihaspati, the Lord of Magic Wisdom, Indra's spiritual adviser, who, with a wizard's smile, took her hand and led her to her husband's throne. There bowing before his majesty, the two settled on the floor before him, where Bṛihaspati, the Lord of Language, commenced a golden discourse on the art of experiencing in the bond of married love the bliss transcending duality. The king and his queen drank in the golden words, which were as a healing balm to their hearts. Indra relented in his extreme resolve. Shachī recovered her radiant joy. And Bṛihaspati promised to compose for them a handbook on the mystery of marriage, wooing ever anew in the knowledge of each as both, to the end of time. [1]

And so the wonderful story ends of the opening of the eyes of an unknowing, self-loving god to a dimension of being, transcendent of himself. Smitten by the full blast of the revelation delivered by two divinities, of a range of consciousness infinitely beyond that required for the competent performance of his own limited historical assignment, bewildered Indra had been about to desert both his public and his domestic orders of worldly duty for the self-satisfaction of self-dissolution in a mystic rapture of self-identification with the infinite, when by great good fortune he was rescued from the mania by the wit of his beautiful queen.

Viṣṇu the Preserver, the first of the two divinities to have appeared before the complacent god, was an approximate counterpart of classical Apollo, who was also a protector of the dreamlike order of the delicately balanced phenomenal forms of this passing world. As a pedagogue, Viṣṇu appears whenever the universal balance is seriously threatened, as it certainly was in Indra's domain by the overload of ego in its ruling god's notion of himself and of what the world owed him. In the way of a proper teacher, Viṣṇu was careful to let his pupil know that the message he was about to learn might be more than he could tolerate. However, with his pride already broken, the secondary god asked humbly to be taught.

Śiva the Destroyer, who in the instructive tale appeared in the character of Hairy, is the Indian form of that Neolithic god of the generative power of nature who in Greece appeared as Dionysos. [2] As a god of the wilderness and the untamed beasts that inhabit it, Śiva is Lord of the Lingam (the *phallos),* which is symbolic of his generative power, and at the same time, the Lord of Yoga, those psychological disciplines in the ruthless practice of which the mystic, released from attachment to his individual life, is identified with the consciousness of which life and the lives that life consumes are the reflection.

The palace priest Bṛihaspati, the master of metaphorical speech, to whom the beautiful Queen Shachī turned in desperation for assistance, brought the whole burden of his art to the correction of the preposterous situation. For it is the function of the priest to represent the claims of life in the world, ethics against metaphysics, the art of living in the knowledge of transcendence without dissolving into it in a rapture of self-indulgence. Carl Jung somewhere has written that the function of religion is to protect us from an experience of God. Some fifty percent of the mythic tales in Ovid's *Metamorphoses* are of characters, ill-prepared, who were unfavorably transformed by encounters with divinities, the full blast of whose light they were unready to absorb. The priest's practical maxims and metaphorical rites moderate transcendent light to secular conditions, intending harmony and enrichment, not disquietude and dissolution. In contrast, the mystic deliberately offers himself to the blast and may go to pieces.

Like the priest, the artist is a master of metaphorical language. The priest, however, is vocationally committed to a vocabulary already coined, of which he is the representative. He is a performing artist executing scripts already perfectly wrought, and his art is in the execution. Creative artists, in contrast, are creative only insofar as they are innovative. And of their innovations, two degrees are readily distinguished. One, the more immediately obvious, has to do with technical innovations; the other with innovative insights. It is to the latter, of course, that the title of this chapter is intended to refer, and it was to the latter, also, that our opening reference to the mystic way was intended to apply. For the reality to which the artist and the mystic are exposed is, in fact, the same. It is of their own inmost truth brought to consciousness: by the mystic, in direct confrontation, and by the artist, through reflection in the masterworks of his art. The fact that the nature of the artist (as a microcosm) and the nature of the universe (as the macrocosm) are two aspects of the same reality (respectively, as a minute part of the whole, experienced from within, and as the whole, viewed from without—equivalent, respectively, to Schopenhauer's "world as will" and "world as spectacle or idea") accounts sufficiently for that creative interplay of discovery and recognition which alerts the artist to the possibility of a revelatory composition in which outer and inner realities are recognized as the same.

In his early novel *A Portrait of the Artist As a Young Man* (written 1904–1914, published 1916), James Joyce quotes Thomas Aquinas to the effect that "beautiful things are those that please when seen" *(pulcra sunt quae visa placent)*.[3] Beauty is thus a value, a good, an end in itself. Ugliness depresses, beauty exhilarates, heightening the sense of life, which again is a good in itself. Normally art aspires to beauty and thus to a sensuous glorification of life: so that Nietzsche could write of the esthetics of art as "nothing but applied physiology."[4] Whereas *l'art pour l'art,* in his view, was an aberration of the "Decadence" of his century: "the virtuosic croaking of cold-blooded frogs, despairing in their swamp."[5]

Beauty we may regard, then, as a normal and proper intention of the Way of Art, affirmative in its sensuous glorification of life, and thus grounded in physiology. To this degree, the Way of Art coincides with the Way of Beauty. However, there is another and further possible degree or range of the revelation of art that is beyond beauty, namely, the sublime, which has been defined as "that which arouses sentiments of awe and reverence and a sense of vastness and power outreaching human comprehension."[6] Cosmic space and great distances may be experienced as sublime; also, detonations of prodigious power. If beauty so heightens our sense of life that esthetics may be termed "applied physiology," the sublime, transcending physical definitions, suggests magnitudes exceeding life; not refuting, but augmenting life. And from this perspective, viewing art, the same Nietzsche declared: "Art is the proper task of life, art is life's metaphysical exercise.... Art is more worth than truth."[7]

Of the many statements by practicing artists of the first principles of their craft, the most lucid, concise, and helpful that I have been able to find is that of James Joyce in the last chapter of his novel just named, where he distinguishes between what he refers to as "proper" and "improper" art. The latter, in his construction, is art in the service of functions that are not properly, distinctively, and singularly of art. In the words of the young poet Stephen Dedalus, who in the novel is the author's alter ego: "Art is the human disposition of sensible or intelligible matter for an esthetic end."[8]

An essential detail here is the word "intelligible," by which our understanding of the Way of Art is extended to include an order of beauty beyond the immediately sensible, which is of matter beyond perception, purely conceptual, apprehensible by the intellect only, and yet disposed for an *esthetic* end. The word is from the Greek *aisthētikos* ("perceptive"; *aisthanesthai,* "to perceive, to feel") and so has to do with sense experience, but also with feeling. So that "proper" art, in Joyce's view, whether of sensible or of intelligible matter, rests in esthetical, disinterested perception, apprehension, and feeling, whereas "improper" art is in the service of interests other than the esthetic—for example, ethics, economics, sociology, or politics.

Improper art is of two orders: art that excites desire for the represented object, and art that arouses loathing or fear of it. Art that excites desire, Joyce calls pornographic. All advertising art is in this sense pornographic, since it is intended that the viewer should desire to possess in some manner the object represented. Portraits are pornographic if they are no more than likenesses, intended rather to relate the mind in memory to the person (or animal) portrayed than to hold the eye and sentiments to the picture itself, within its frame. Likewise, a landscape that is of interest rather as the advertisement or souvenir of some noteworthy place than as an esthetically engaging organization of sensible matter within a bounded field is in Joyce's sense pornographic. In India, as already noticed (see page 6), such works are characterized as *deśī* ("popular, local, provincial") and regarded as esthetically insignificant.

Art that arouses loathing or fear, Joyce terms didactic. Derogatory satire, portrayal, and social criticism are didactic and therefore, in Joyce's sense, improper art. Fascist and Marxist art is, of course, deliberately didactic; but in Europe and America as well, since the period of Émile Zola (1840–1902), sociopolitical didacticity has in many quarters become regarded even as the sole justification of art, which is otherwise "escapist" and "ivory tower."

All "improper" art, whether pornographic or didactic, thus moves one, or at least is meant to move one, to action, either with desire toward the object, or with fear or loathing *away* from it. It is therefore, as Joyce says, *kinetic* (Greek, *kinetikos,* from *kinein,* "to move"), whereas "proper" art is static (Greek, *statikos,* "causing to stand"). We speak of esthetic arrest. One is not moved to physical action of any kind, but held in sensational (esthetic) contemplation and enjoyment. In Joyce's words: "The mind is arrested and raised above desire and loathing."9

It is this elevation of mind and, with the mind, the eye, above desire and loathing, desire and fear, that brings the way of art and the artist into relation to that of the mystic. Without this transformation at once of consciousness and of vision, the portal of the mansion of art has not been entered. Studio techniques alone, not only are of no use, but also may mislead even the gifted craftsman himself. Likewise on the mystic way, the acquisition of fantastic psychophysiological powers through yoga may lead the practitioner astray. This point is made in many Hindu legends telling of demons who by dint of extreme perseverance in yoga attained to such extraordinary powers *(siddhi)* that they were able to overthrow the ruling gods and gain control of the universe. Vṛitra (the "Encloser") in the tale "The Humbling of Indra" (pages 20–25) was such a monster. And the effect upon the world of his reign was the creation of a universal Waste Land. Likewise, the effect upon the world today of the preponderancy in the popular mind of journalistic sociopolitical didacticism laced with pornographic entertainment (expiring Rome's "bread and circuses," *panem et circenses)* has been to release over the planet in this century the Four Horsemen of the Apocalypse (Revelation 6:1–7). What thunderblast of the spirit must be launched to blow this multiheaded Lord of the Century to smithereens?

The blast will not make a lot of noise, nor will it break upon us all at once. In fact, the conditions for its coming are already here. As viewed by astronauts from the moon, the earth lacks those lines of sociopolitical division that are so prominent on maps. And as recognized here below, the web of interlacing socioeconomic interdependencies that now infolds the planet is of one life. All that is required is a general change of vision to accord with these contemporary facts. And that this will occur is certain. It is, in fact, already occurring. Moreover, the vision required is nothing new, nor unnatural. What are unnatural, artificial and contrived, are the separations.

Already in the nineteenth century, on the untamed Western Plains, a Native American, Black Elk (see pages 7–8), in a shamanic vision of himself standing on the summit of the central mountain of the world—which, as he then knew, was everywhere, though for himself, locally, it was Harney Peak, South Dakota—saw that the sacred hoop of his people was one of many hoops that made one circle wide as daylight and as starlight.[10] Indeed, the idea is fully and even elegantly represented in the Great Seal of the United States, which appears engraved on the back of every dollar bill in our wallets.

There (see Figure 16) at the summit of a symbolic pyramid (the World Mountain) we see an eye within a radiant, upward-pointing triangle (the World Eye, God's Eye, Eye of Spirit). It is at that point of rest *(stasis)* at the summit where the opposed sides come together. Above it is an inscription: *Annuit coeptis,* "He or It (God, the Eye) has smiled on our undertakings" (which is adapted from Virgil's *Aeneid* IX.625). Below, displayed on a scroll, is another inscription: *Novus ordo seclorum,* "A new order of the world." And along the base of the pyramid is a date, 1776, in Roman numerals. Across the bill is an American bald eagle, bearing in its beak a scroll with the inscription *E pluribus unum,* "Out of many, one" (see Figure 17). Above its head is a radiant solar disk enclosing the thirteen stars of the original thirteen states (thirteen being a number signifying transcendence through a spiritual transformation). The stars are symmetrically arranged to suggest the six-pointed symbol known as Solomon's Seal, or Star of David, which in India appears in the heart *cakra, cakra* 4 of the *kuṇḍalinī,* the center of spiritual awakening (see Figure 3 and pages 36–37), where it is symbolic of the spiritual condition of one who is, in life, enlightened. For the upward-pointing triangle is of the spiritual eye (compare the eye above the pyramid), the downward-pointing triangle being of the claims of this temporal world. And the bald eagle is a local American form of the solar eagle, the bird and vehicle of Zeus, symbolic here of the mode of action in the field of time of a people inspired by the spirit. War and peace are represented by the arrows and laurel spray in the bird's talons, left and right, and the turn of the bird's head is to the laurel.

The vision of Black Elk on the symbolic summit of Harney Peak, "seeing in a sacred manner," as he declared, "the shapes of all things in the spirit, and the shape of all things as they must live together, like one being," had been achieved in *the mystic way* by an especially gifted shaman. In contrast, the elegant eighteenth-century engraving still to be seen on the back of our twentieth-century dollar bill represents a realization of *the philosophical way* pursued by that extraordinary company of deists to whom we owe the establishment, in reason, of this nation. Composed of elements adapted from a hermetic tradition of great antiquity and universality (undoubtedly assembled from the library and great learning of Thomas Jefferson), its pictorial vocabulary is so little understood today that many suppose the word "God" of its maxim, "In God we trust," to be a reference to the "God" of the Christian religion, which it is not. For the deists rejected the idea of the

"Fall" and, with that, the necessity for "Redemption," as well as the idea of a special Judeo-Christian revelation. Man's nature, in their view, is not corrupt. The idea of God is innate in man's mind from the beginning; so that by reason alone man has arrived, everywhere, at a recognition of God which is sufficient. Religious intolerance is blasphemy, since in their primal ground and ultimate sense, all religions are one, as is mankind.

The way of art, when followed "properly" (in Joyce's sense), leads also to the mountaintop that is everywhere, beyond opposites, of transcendental vision, where, as Blake discovered and declared, "the doors of perception are cleansed and every thing appears to man as it is, infinite." [11] The engraving on the back of the dollar bill delivers its message as a work of art: in the way, however, of an illustration of concepts already formed, not as an affective, unprecedented image in itself. Many works of religious art are of this kind. They illustrate legends already known, of saints, angels, incarnations, and the like, and they commonly contain, like the deist engraving on the back of the dollar bill, standard symbolic devices which are addressed, not to the eye, but through the eye to the intellect, the meanings of which can be known only to those already familiar with the illustrated tradition. Such a composition may grace the eye, but in itself it lacks magic, or, as Joyce would say, the "radiance" *(claritas)* of an achieved work of "proper" art. One's heart is waked, not by the form of the work, but by its content, and if the latter is of a tradition either unknown or deceased, the work may be of interest, like the dollar bill, economically, but it is no longer a work of living art.

Figure 16. Reverse, Great Seal of the United States.

The Eye of the Holy Spirit, here shown at the summit of a Pyramid of Creation, is a counterpart of the Eye of Viṣṇu mentioned in the Indian tale of the "Humbling of Indra" (page 25). One may think of it as connoting, metaphorically, that mysterious "impulse" out of which the Big Bang of creation sent flying into distances that are still receding in expanding space, hundreds of millions of exploding atomic furnaces which are seen from this earth as stars, constellations, and a Milky Way of innumerable points of light (see pages 2–3).

The present pyramid is not, however, of that first creation, but of a second, a "new order of the world" *(novus ordo seclorum),* represented here as constituted of exactly 13 courses

allegorical of our 13 original states. And whereas behind the new pyramid there is only a desert to be seen, before and around it are the sprouting signs of a new and fresh beginning, dated 1776: 1 + 7 + 7 + 6 = 21. Mankind, that is to say, has herewith come of age and taken to itself responsibility and authority for the shaping of human lives according to Reason.

Moreover, between the dated course at the pyramid's base, which tells of an occurrence in Time, and the Eye at the top, which is of Eternity, there are 12 courses, this being the number of signs of the belt of the zodiac as defining the limits of the physical world. The number 13, accordingly, which is that of the dated course at the base, represents a creative transcendence of the boundary: not death, as appears in the popular superstition of 13 at table, but an achieved life beyond death, as signified in the model of the table of the Last Supper, where the 12 Apostles were of the number of the signs of the belt of the zodiac by which the physical world is bounded, whereas the incarnate God who was about to die, though indeed among them in the field of Time, was of Eternity, beyond the pale of death. Thus the number 13 of our 13 originating states is here interpreted and celebrated as the sign of a resurrection of life out of death, fresh leaves from a desert, a wholesome gift of the light of Reason as an awakener to maturity of the mind in its social conscience.

Figure 17. Obverse, Great Seal of the United States.

In the radiant disk above the American bald eagle's head the stars of the original 13 states are composed to form a Solomon's Seal symbolic of the union of soul and body, spirit and matter. Each of the interlaced equilateral triangles, one upward turned, the other downward, is a Pythagorean *tetraktys,* or "perfect triangle of fourness," of nine points, four to a side, enclosing a tenth representing the generative center ("still point of the turning world") out of which the others derive their force. The upward triangle is of spiritual, the downward pointing, of physical energy. Thus interlaced, the two represent the physical world recognized as informed by the spiritual, and in exactly this sense they appear at the Lotus Center of the awakened heart, *cakra* 4, in the symbolic Lotus series of the Indian *kuṇḍalinī* (Figure 3, page 37).

In the Classical imagination, the 9 circumferential points of the Pythagorean *tetraktys* were identified with the Muses and the point in the center with Apollo, around whose radiant form the 9 dance. In Jewish thought, the sign of the two triangles together is known as "magen david" (Hebrew, *māghēn Dāwīdh),* "Shield of David," and read as connoting the *shekhīnāh,* or presence of God in Israel (as originally in the burning bush and in the cloud on the summit of Mt. Sinai). In the Great Seal of the United States the reference is to the inspiration of the light of Reason in the constitution of the originating 13 colonies brought together as one nation: *e pluribus unum,* "out of many, one." These are homologous, though culturally differentiated, interpretations of the same "elementary idea."

When viewed as outlining a pyramid, the upward pointing triangle matches the pyramid on the reverse of the Seal, with the single point at its apex corresponding to the Eye out of which the expanding form of the universe has proceeded. As symbolized in the traditional Pythagorean *tetraktys,* the energy emanating from that initial point (which is of the opening both from and to Eternity) yields, first, duality (*2 points:* measure and chaos, subject and object, light and dark, odd and even, male and female, etc.), which then relate to each other in three ways (*3 points:* either *a* dominant, *b* dominant, or *a* and *b* in accord), whence derive all the phenomenal forms in the field of space-time (*4 points:* 4 quarters of the earth and heavens). There is a verse in the Chinese *Tao Teh Ching:* "The Tao produced One; One produced Two; Two produced Three; Three produced All things" (*Tao Teh Ching* 42, translation, James Legge). Thus the ancient symbolism of the *tetraktys:* 1 point, 2 points, 3 points, and 4; which series when read in the opposite sense, of ascending or returning to the source, yields the interesting series, 4 3 2 (for the sense of which, see pages 9-13).

Connotations of the same order pertain, of course, to the downward turned *tetraktys,* with its single point at the apex opening also from and to Eternity; so that "what is above is below," and the energy of the Spirit (however named), whether from without (as from the Eye, the apex above) or from within the world (the apex below) is one. Moreover, since from every terminal point of the six-pointed Solomon's Seal the same increasing series of 2 to 3 to 4 proceeds, it follows that the intended sense of the radiant symbol of 13 stars above the American bald eagle's head must have been the same essentially as that of Black Elk's remark, "The center is everywhere" (see pages 7-8)—above and below, north, south, east,

and west—with an additional eighteenth-century implication of the humanizing fight of Reason reflected, universally, in the clarified consciousness of mankind.

The number of stripes on the American eagle's shield is 13; so also the number of the arrows and of the leaves of the laurel spray in its talons, while the number of the feathers of its tail is 9 (see page 11).

The artist fashioning a work of this kind serves in the way, rather, of the priest of an assured tradition than of an innovating creator, and the refinement of his vocabulary can be astounding. Consider, for instance, the elegant concision of the statement of the relationship of a theological ground to the polity of this nation, founded in benevolence and reason, that is represented in the ideogram of the outspread eagle on our dollar bill (Figure 17): overhead, the twofold *tetraktys* arranged in the form of a Solomon's Seal of thirteen five-pointed stars; other recurrences of the number 13; the sum of the feathers in the eagle's tail (3 + 3 + 3); and the offered choices of either a spray of laurel or a sheaf of 13 arrows. It is ironical that today we should be passing around as legal tender these sociological manifestos without being able to read the message of democracy engraved on every one of them, the spiritual inspiration out of which their economic value has been derived. So that, not only the message, but even its vocabulary, have been lost.

But also lost has been the power of all such recondite, iconographic art to melt the mind, enchant the heart, and cast a spell of esthetic arrest. For there has been a vast transformation of consciousness, not only in the Western world, but over the whole face of the earth, in the two brief centuries that have elapsed since the dating in Roman numerals of that pyramid.

James Joyce, in *A Portrait of the Artist As a Young Man,* like every one of those young artists of his time who, during the century that has now run its course, became the masters of the period, put his mind to the problem of reawakening the eye and heart to wonder. With the profound sense of a call, a vocation, he turned his mind (like the ancient Greek master craftsman Daedalus, when he found himself entrapped in a labyrinth of his own fashioning) to the invention of a hitherto unknown science of escape from bondage on "wings of art." And for instruction in the manufacture of such wings, he turned to Aristotle and to Aristotle's medieval disciple, Aquinas:

"Aquinas says," states Stephen Dedalus, *"Ad pulcritundinem tria requiruntur, integritas, consonantia, claritas.* I translate it so: *Three things are needed for beauty, wholeness, harmony, and radiance."* [12]

Integritas (wholeness): To appreciate the effect of this principle, the function of which is to create an enclosed hermetic field of self-defined and self-defining, impractical relationships, one may regard any collection of objects whatsoever, say a clutter of things on a table, and in imagination put a frame around them. Everything within the frame is now to be regarded as *one thing*, not as a collection of unrelated objects of various use, but as the related parts of a composition. Those parts, say, of the table or of any of the other objects that are outside the frame are now "other," and what is within the frame is one thing. "You see it," says Stephen, "as a whole. You apprehend its wholeness. That is *integritas.*" [13]

Consonantia (harmony): What is now important, and *all* that is now important, is whether this object or that is here, or *there:* the relationship of part to part, of each part to the whole, and of the whole to each of its parts. *This is the esthetic instrument: rhythm, consonantia.* The parts may be objects, colors, words and their sounds, musical intervals, architectural features and proportions. "You pass," says Stephen, "from point to point, led by its formal lines; you apprehend it as balanced part against part within its limits; you feel the rhythm of its structure."[14]

Claritas (radiance): When the rhythm has been fortunately struck, one is held to it in delight, with no sense of any other use for it. "You see that it is that thing which it is and no other thing," declares Stephen. "The radiance of which [Aquinas] speaks is the scholastic *quidditas,* the *whatness* of a thing. This supreme quality is felt by the artist when the esthetic image is first conceived in his imagination. The mind in that mysterious instant Shelley likened beautifully to a fading coal. The instant wherein that supreme quality of beauty, the clear radiance of the esthetic image, is apprehended luminously by the mind which has been arrested by its wholeness and fascinated by its harmony is the luminous silent stasis of esthetic pleasure, a spiritual state very like to that cardiac condition which the Italian physiologist Luigi Galvani, using a phrase almost as beautiful as Shelley's, called the enchantment of the heart."[15]

And this surely is the justification of art, its healing force and its wonder: that beauty apprehended should have this power to illuminate the senses, still the mind, and enchant the heart. "Art," Cézanne has said somewhere, "is a harmony parallel to nature." And I recall having heard the sculptor Antoine Bourdelle declare, as one of his maxims: *"L'art fait ressortir les grandes lignes de la nature."* For nature, as we know, is at once without and within us. Art is the mirror at the interface. So too is ritual; so also myth. These, too, "bring out the grand lines of nature," and in doing so, reestablish us in our own deep truth, which is at one with that of all being.

So that the artist, functioning in this "proper" way, is the true seer and prophet of his century, the justifier of life and as such, of course, a revolutionary far more fundamental in his penetration of the social mask of his day than any fanatic idealist spilling blood over the pavement in the name simply of another unnatural mask.

Wholeness, harmony, and radiance, then, are the prime requirements of any work of what Joyce would term proper art. In its own space, the object or composition is set apart as a thing of beauty in its own nature, which is experienced as akin to that of the witness. There is a telling moment of impact when this recognition strikes, and one is held as by the mystery of one's own face in a glass. Therewith, the radiance. When the object is another living being, this recognition is empathic, and where suffering, physical or mental, is represented (as in tragedy) the heart opens to compassion.

Stephen Dedalus, addressing himself to this last type and degree of esthetic arrest, turns for guidance to Aristotle, in whose *Poetics* the tragic emotions named are pity and terror. "Aristotle," says Stephen, "has not defined pity and terror. I have." And he proceeds to his definitions (the italics following are mine):

"Pity is the feeling which *arrests* the mind in the presence of whatsoever is grave and *constant* in human sufferings and unites it with the *human* sufferer." Not the poor, the black, the jobless sufferer, be it noted, but the human sufferer. We are penetrating the local, ethnic, or social mask to the human being.

"Terror is the feeling which *arrests* the mind in the presence of whatsoever is grave and *constant* in human sufferings and unites it with the *secret* cause."[16] Here we are moving toward an experience of the sublime. What is the secret cause of any moment of suffering? (This is the problem that the Buddha formulated as his First Noble Truth: "All life is sorrowful.") Let us consider an example.

Mr. A shoots and kills Mr. B. What is the *secret* cause of B's death? Is it the bullet? That is the instrumental, moving, or efficient cause. If we are writing about bullets, we may produce a tract on gun control, but it will not be a work of proper art. Or let us say that Mr. A is a white man and Mr. B a black man. Is the secret cause of B's death racial conflict in the United States? If that is what we are writing about, the product may be an important novel of social criticism, but it will not be properly a tragedy or even a work of proper art.

What, then, is the secret cause of Mr. B's death?

I have chosen the illustration of a black man and a white man with the death in mind specifically of Martin Luther King, Jr., on April 4, 1968, and with the brave words in mind that were reported of him shortly before the assassination, when he declared that he knew that by persisting in his populist crusade for justice, peace, and righteousness he was challenging, not simply opposition, but possible assassination; yet he pressed on. For here is a clue to the secret cause.

In Aristotle's *Poetics,* tragedy is analyzed as a form of dramatic composition in which the leading character is by some passion or limitation brought to a catastrophe.

But every life, either knowingly or unknowingly, is in process toward its limitation in death, which limitation is of the nature of life. Moreover, every significant act sets up a counterfield of resistance, in the way of the Buddhist doctrine of "dependent origination, or mutual arising" (*pratītya-samutpāda*). Opposites arise by mutual consent; so that the stronger the passion of one, the closer the limitation of the other. Dame Prudence advises care to the principle of limitation, tempering one's passion for life to the imminency of King Death. But the heroic life of deeds and fame is of the one whose passion bends Death's margin to the limit. In a work of "improper" art, such an assassination as that of Martin Luther King would have to be represented either as justified or as reprehensible. In a tragedy, in contrast, it would appear as the culminating revelation of the character and value of a lifetime; and since a work of "proper" art cannot say nay, but only yea, to life in life's celebration, such a death in high career would be, beyond the sorrow of it, affirmed. And in this affirmation itself the mind is carried beyond, purged and cleansed of the fear of death.

The word "catharsis" (Greek *katharsis;* from *kathairein,* "to cleanse"), which in Aristotle's usage denotes the effect of tragedy as "effecting through pity and terror a *katharsis* of these emotions,"[17] was a term which referred in the Greek religious vocabulary to a spiritual transformation brought about by participation in a rite. The mind, "cleansed" of attachments to merely secular aims, desires, and fears, is released to spiritual rapture. Plato writes of *katharsis,* for example, as a "defeat of the sensations of pleasure."[18] The ultimate effect, that is to say, is not to be of beauty (which "when seen pleases"), but of the sublime ("outreaching human comprehension").[19] The Greek theater was throughout its career associated with the shrines and festivals of Dionysos, who was a god, not only of the vine and drunken ecstasy, but also, more fundamentally, of the generative power of all life, the will in nature. His Hindu counterpart, as we have already said, is Śiva, whom we have lately met in the character of Hairy (see pages 24–25), and like Śiva, Dionysos was a god at once of the wilderness and its untamed beasts, the phallus, and spiritual transport through "enthusiasm" (from the Greek *enthusiazein,* "to be inspired or possessed by a god"). The Indian tantric saying *nādevo devam arcayet,* "by none but a god shall a god be worshiped," is a text speaking to this same state of possession. The art of the Greek tragedies of the fifth century B.C., which were composed for and presented during the Great Dionysia at Athens, had originated from rhapsodic celebrations of the force of this universal deity's immanence, and hence influence, through every part of the web of human life.

As James Joyce in the character of Stephen Dedalus perceived, however, the description by Aristotle of the means by which the Greek tragedians rendered to their audiences an affective experience of their god's immanence through every phase of the action of their plots remains unclear, because he did not (at least in the imperfect text of his *Poetics* that has come down to us) define pity and terror. Classical historians have, as a consequence, for the past 2,300 years, confused his "pity and terror" with desire and fear, interpreting *katharsis,* accordingly, as a "cleansing out" of pity and terror by means of a large dose of the same. But surely the mystical aim of the earlier rites can never have been to get rid of, but rather to inspire, pity and terror; for these are the two preeminent religious sentiments. What was to be achieved was a voiding of secular desire and loathing (or fear) by a transformation of consciousness. Desire and loathing (or fear) are *kinetic.* They motivate the mind and feelings in relation to phenomenal appearances, moving one either to possess or to reject them. Pity and terror, on the contrary, are *static.* Pity (or perhaps better, compassion) arises in the recognition of shared humanity. In the drama this occurs in relation to the characters on stage. Moreover, the sufferings revealed through the episodes of a tragedy are not accidental or occasional, but "grave and constant," archetypal of human life. Thus a breakthrough is accomplished from biography to metaphysics, the backdrop of time dissolves and the prospect opens of an occult power shaping our lives that is at once of the universe and of each of us, a *mysterium tremendum et fascinans,* which is finally that everlasting fire which is exploding in the galaxies, blazing in the sun, reflected in the moon, and coursing as the ache of desire through our veins.

"The way of the mystic and the way of the artist are related, except that the mystic doesn't have a craft."

When the Prince Siddhārtha, Gautama Shakyamuni, rode from his palace in the dead of night on Kanthaka, his magnificent white stallion, with his charioteer, Chandaka, running swiftly at his side, he passed deep into the forest to a hermitage where he dismounted; and Kanthaka, bearing the empty saddle, was conducted back to the palace, where he died of grief.

From one hermitage to another, one teaching sage to another, the future Buddha passed in search of his way. For a time he joined a company of ascetics in a discipline of severe fasting, until with only skin and bone remaining, he considered: "But this certainly is not the way to passionless knowledge and liberation." So he rose and left the fasting. And having bathed, thin as he was, in the lovely stream Nairanjana, supported by the trees along the shore as by a hand, he came back onto the bank. And as he was there resting, Nandabala, the daughter of a leading herdsman of those parts, approached with a rich bowl of milk rice, by which his body was restored. And he rose and, alone, proceeded to the Bodhi tree, where he placed himself on the Immovable Spot, facing east.

Then it was that there appeared before him the lord of the motivating powers of temporal life, whose three names are Kāma ("Desire"), Māra ("Death"), and Dharma ("Social Duty"). And in his first character, as Kāma, the god displayed before the one there seated his three opulent daughters, Desire, Delight, and Pining. But the Blessed One was unmoved.

The god assumed, then, his form inspiring fear, and an army of ogres immediately taking shape around him flung weapons, fire, even mountains at the Blessed One, who remained, however, unmoved. And the hurled weapons became transformed into flower offerings.

So then, finally, as the Lord Dharma of Earthly Duties, the governing god of this world challenged the right of the Blessed One to be seated there, immovable, in disregard of the good of his kingdom. Whereupon, the future Buddha only moved his right hand to touch with its fingertips the earth, when a voice was heard resounding through all the earth and sky: "O Māra, put away thy malice. Go in peace. For never will this Great Being, whose merit has brought him to this central place, abandon his resolve." The god with his daughters and army thereupon vanished, and that night the Blessed One acquired (1) the Eye of Transcendent Vision, (2) knowledge of his Life beyond lives, and (3) comprehension of the Law of Dependent Origination, by which all beings arise in mutual dependency.

He was now, therefore, the "Awakened One," a Buddha (from the root *budh,* of the verb *bodhati,* "he awakes"), and for the next fifty years he remained awakened in the world as a teacher of the mystic way. [20]

One is struck, in reviewing this legend, by the exact coincidence of the names of the Buddha's antagonist with the motivations by which, in Joyce's view, an artist is turned from the "proper" way of his art—namely (1) Kāma ("desire"), (2) Māra ("death"; which is to say, the "fear of death"), and (3) Dharma ("social duties, virtues, and commitments"). Significant, also, is the idea of the Immovable Spot, upon which the future Buddha took his seat to pursue his aim. This corresponds to Black Elk's "center of the world," which is everywhere and from which he viewed "in a sacred manner" all things. It is not a geographical place, but the state of mind of one released from the vortex of delusory desires, fears, and commitments by which lives in this world are compelled to their sorrows and pains. In the words of T. S. Eliot's "Burnt Norton":

> At the still point of the turning world. Neither flesh nor fleshless;
> Neither from nor towards; at the still point, there the dance is,
> But neither arrest nor movement. And do not call it fixity,
> Where the past and future are gathered. Neither movement
>   from nor towards,
> Neither ascent nor decline. Except for the point, the still point,
> There would be no dance, and there is only the dance.
> I can only say, *there* we have been: but I cannot say where.
> And I cannot say, how long, for that is to place it in time.
> The inner freedom from the practical desire,
> The release from action and suffering, release from the inner
> And the outer compulsion, yet surrounded
> By a grace of sense, a white light still and moving... [21]

It is there, which is no "where," that the Eye opens of Transcendent Vision, which in the way of art is of that instant (once again to quote James Joyce) "wherein that supreme quality of beauty, the clear radiance of the esthetic image, is apprehended luminously by the mind which has been arrested by its wholeness and fascinated by its harmony...the luminous silent stasis of esthetic pleasure." [22]

In India, the attainment of this state of mind is the classic aim of yoga.

Variously described, it is known finally as *Nirvāṇa,* which is not to be conceived of, like Heaven, as a place, but as a dying out in the heart of the threefold fire of *rāga, doṣa,* and *moha* ("passion," "hatred," and "delusion"). For the word *vā* means "to blow"; *nir-vā,* "to extinguish, to blow out," and accordingly, *nir-vāṇa* means, literally, "blown out, gone out, disappeared." What has been "blown out"? In relation to the idea of reincarnation, what has been "blown out" is the impulse and need to be born again; so that in this sense one may say that life (as future life) has been blown out. However, in relation to the present incarnation, it has not been life, but desire, loathing or fear, and the ignorance or delusion that they inspire and represent, which have been blown out. And since these, as we have found, are exactly the *kinetic* traits that Joyce identifies with improper art, whereas proper art is of the *static* state of the mind and eye that have been "arrested and raised above" these conditioning factors by which vision is prejudiced and actuality overshaded, it follows that the way of the mystic and the way of the "proper" artist are indeed related.

In fact, in the Orient they are identical, except that the mystic doesn't have a craft. For, as Ananda K. Coomaraswamy has stated in one of his numerous treatments of this subject: "the practice of art [in India] is a discipline *(yoga)* beginning with attention *(dharaṇa),* consummated in self-identification *(samādhi),* viz. with the object or theme of contemplation, and eventuating in skill of operation *(kauśala)."* [23] Assumed from the beginning is the metaphysical principle announced already in the Chhāndogya Upaniṣad (c. ninth century B.C.), "thou art that" *(tat tvam asi),* which is to say, thou art, in truth, a form of that same transcendent consciousness of which all phenomena, physical as well as psychical, are forms. Consequently, as Heinrich Zimmer observed in his first masterwork, *Kunstform und Yoga im indischen Kultbild* (Berlin, 1926), which is now at last available in English: "For Indian art, man is god, and art is created so that he might experience this truth and need art no longer.... Its raison d'être lies in the fact that it points beyond itself: it can appear as essence only to someone limited by Ignorance *(avidyā),* Not-yet-enlightened *(a-pra-buddha):* 'For the Brahmin versed in sacrifice and the Vedic texts, God is in fire; for the worshiper, in his own heart; for the Not-yet-enlightened, in the sacred image; but for him who is aware of the highest Self, God is in All Things.'" [24]

Emphatically, therefore, the accent in Indian art is not upon the welter of images before one's eyes, but on the background of an unseen power *(brahman)* or void *(śunyaīā),* over which they dance. For they are of the delusive veil of *māyā,* magical apparitions, bursting as foam from the breaking waves of a cosmic sea, which in its depth is still.

There is among the surviving documents of early-medieval India's golden Gupta age of literature and art (fourth to sixth centuries A.D.), a work on dramaturgy, the *Daśarūpa,* of Dhanaṃjaya,[25] in which the aim of the dramatic art is described as the communication of "enjoyment" *(svāda)* by rendering "sentiments, tastes, or flavors" *(rasa),* there being five kinds of "enjoyment" and nine "sentiments" or "flavors." "As for any simple man of little intelligence," we read at the opening of this work, "who says that from dramas which distill joy, the gain is knowledge only, as in the case of history and the like, homage to him, for he has averted his face from what is delightful."[26] "Whether one take a subject that is delightful or disgusting, exalted or lowly, cruel or kindly, obscure (as in the original story) or adapted (to be more intelligible), or whether one take a subject originated by the imagination of a poet, there is no subject that cannot succeed in conveying Sentiment *(rasa)* among mankind."[27]

Rasa, then, is the effectual agent of this art, the word meaning, literally, "sap or juice, nectar, liquid, water, drink"; metaphorically, "essence"; and in relation to works of art, "beauty." The nine *rasas* named in the *Daśarūpa* as pertaining to the drama have been assigned as follows to the five *svādas,* or "enjoyments."

I. Cheerfulness
The Erotic and the Comic

II. Exaltation
The Heroic and the Marvelous

III. Agitation
The Odious and the Terrible

IV. Perturbation of Mind
The Furious and the Pathetic

V. Happiness in Tranquility
The Peaceful

The last is not, like the others, to be separately developed in distinct compositions, but to underlie the experiences of all as a kind of drone, or ground, over which they play. It is an experience of the "permanent state" *(śthāyin-bhāva)* known as *sāma* ("peace of mind"), which is characterized by "tranquility, indifference to the objects of sense, and repose in the knowledge of *brahman.*"[28]

Of the *svādas,* the closest to the Greek idea of tragedy is number IV. "Perturbation of Mind," as represented in dramas of the furious *(raudra)* and pathetic *(karuṇa)* sentiments. *Raudra* ("wrathful, violent, terrible") is a term affiliated with the name *Rudra* ("Howling, Roaring") of the Vedic god of storms, who became in later thought associated with Śiva as Destroyer. But Śiva, we have seen, is the Indian counterpart of Dionysos, patron god of the Greek tragedy (pages 90–91). So that the term corresponds in sense about as closely as could be wished to Joyce's understanding of Aristotle's "tragic terror"; while *karuṇa,* "that which causes pity" (pity or compassion, *karuṇā),* corresponds to "tragic pity." The *Daśarūpa* is of a date nearly a thousand years later than Aristotle's *Poetics,* and that there was a massive classical influence upon Gupta thought and art cannot be doubted.[29] However, that the means must have greatly differed by which pity and terror were communicated in ancient Greece and medieval India, I can testify, as having witnessed in New Delhi a production of Sophocles' *Oedipus Rex,* where the audience was rather appalled than enchanted by the carnality of the plot and characterizations; for there is nothing of the fairy tale about the atmosphere of a Greek tragedy, no sense of the play of *māyā* to disengage the reality of the characters from their histories. There is no subliminal ground of repose in *brahman,* over which the passions, limitations, and catastrophes of the action play, like the figurations of a dream. The release in a Greek tragedy comes, rather, at the end of the piece, in the minds of the audience, as a transformation of perspective.

Indian dramas of Type Number I, affording "Cheerfulness" through enjoyment of the Erotic *(śriṅgāra)* and Comic *(hāsya)* sentiments, are best represented in the poet Kālidāsa's classic masterpiece, *Śakuntalā Recognized (Abhijñānaśakuntalā),* which in 1789 appeared in English as the first work of Sanskrit dramatic writing translated into any Western tongue; of which Goethe then wrote the oft-quoted lines:

If you wish the blossom of the early and fruit of the late years,
Wish what is charming and exciting, as well as nourishing and sub-
stantial.
Wish to capture in one name heaven and earth:
I name for you, Shakuntala, and all is said.[30]

In keeping with the classic prescriptions of this art, the source of delight in Kālidāsa's play is of a single archetypal, or "Permanent State"
(sthāyin-bhāva), which is maintained without interference throughout, in-
flected through modifications, balanced by a supporting, secondary state,
and illustrated in every situation. The "permanent state" in this case is
"love" *(rati),* which appears, not only as the infatuation of a king in a
young woman of high birth discovered in a forest hermitage, but also as
Śakuntalā's love for the forest and its creatures, and of the animals for the
gentle girl; of the king for his subjects and the people for their king; worshipers for their deity and the order of nature itself for its children of good-
will. Love saturates the atmosphere, gracefully complemented by the
secondary permanent state of Mirth *(hāsa).* And the plot is, of course, of
Infatuation, Separation, and Reunion. As summarized in the *Daśarūpa:*
"Just as a verb...when combined with nouns relating to it, is the essence
of a sentence, so a Permanent State, when combined with other states, is
the essence of a play."[31]

Type Number II of dramatic enjoyment, "Exaltation" derived from
plays of the Heroic *(vīra)* and Marvelous *(adbhuta)* sentiments, medieval
Europe knew in its Germanic and Celtic epics, out of which Wagner drew
the matter of his *Ring des Nibelungen* (1853–74) and *Parsifal* (1882). The
Sanskrit term, *vīra* ("mighty, brave, heroic"; also, "warrior, champion,
hero") is related, both etymologically and in meaning, to English "virile"
(Latin *virilis,* "manly," and *vir,* "adult male"; compare Old High German
wer and Old Irish *fer).* The word "virtue" (Latin *virtus)* was also of this
family in its earlier sense of "excellence" of any kind, "capacity" or
"power" to effect results, which is to say, in its earlier, heroic sense. With
the later shift in the understanding of "virtue" to "conformity to a
Christian moral code," which Nietzsche discussed in his *Genealogy of
Morals* (1887), the heroic arts lost favor in the West (last stand in
Cervantes's *Don Quixote,* early sixteenth century) and have survived only

in the reflected way of the romantic nostalgia (as in Wagner) for an age of incredible deeds in a fabulous past. The Sanskrit term *adbhuta* ("marvelous, surprising, supernatural, transcendental") lets us know that the deeds were not to have been taken literally, but poetically, as metaphorical of powers to be cherished of the human spirit. But even as metaphor, they are no longer positively regarded. In fact, we in America have a literature even of the anti-hero, best represented, and most "marvelously" *(adbhuta)*, 1918–1940, in Charlie Chaplin.

Finally, Enjoyment Type Number III. "Agitation," of the "Odious" *(bībhatsa)* and "Terrible" *(bhayānaka)* sentiments, would seem to represent the Indian state of mind most closely related to that of not a little of the modern arts. The meanings of the two Sanskrit terms, *bībhatsa,* "loathsome, nauseous, hideous, detestable"; also, "cruel, envious, and wicked," and then, *bhayānaka,* "fearsome, frightful, terrible, horrible, terrific," set the intended sentiments distinctly apart from those of Type IV, the Furious *(raudra)* and the Pathetic *(karuṇa),* since, in the first place, there is nothing here of compassion *(karuṇā),* while in the second place, whereas the term *raudra* suggests the "fury and anger" of a raging god (namely, Rudra, Śiva in his terrific aspect), the term *bhayānaka* is of the "permanent state," not of "wrath" *(krodha),* but of "fear" *(bhaya).* So that the two states represented are, respectively, of "disgust" *(jugupsā)* and "fear" *(bhaya),* which brings us dangerously close to Joyce's definition of improper art—except that in this art there is no didacticism. The aim is not "knowledge or the like," but "enjoyment," and the sentiments rendered are of permanent states, not to be corrected, but to be experienced.

Moreover, in Indian art there is always an intended connotation to be recognized of immanent divinity. As stated in the Bhagavad Gītā by Kṛṣṇa (Krishna), the teaching incarnation of Viṣṇu the Preserver: "The one, yoked in yoga, viewing alike all beings, discerns the Self in all, and all beings in the Self. When he thus perceives me in everything and everything in me, I shall not be lost to him, nor will he be lost to me."[32] So that, finally, all rests well, all struggle and all conflict, in God, the Lord.

That is the Enjoyment Type Number V. "Happiness in Tranquility," which, as already noted, is not separately developed in distinct compositions, but underlies all as a kind of drone over which they play. Its "permanent state" is *sāma,* "peace of mind," which is characterized by "tranquility, indifference to the objects of sense, and repose in the knowledge of *brahman,*" while the "sentiment," or *rasa,* by which the realization is flavored is the "peaceful" *(sānta-rasa),* the experience of which is an effect simply of the harmonious composition of the work of art: what Joyce would have called its "rhythm of beauty," *consonantia,* its relation of part to part, of each part to the whole, and of the whole to each of its parts. Set apart, within its own frame, from the general context of phenomenality *(integritas),* the composed drama, dance, or epic tale is viewed in the con-texture of its own harmonius arrangement *(consonantia),* where it is recognized by the *rasika* (the appreciator of *rasa,* the viewer, the connoisseur) *a priori,* as a revelation of that Self, which, as we have learned from the Gītā, is the Self *(ātman-brahman)* of all beings. So that Joyce's *quidditas,* or "whatness" of the object of art (see page 101), is exactly, in Indian terms, *brahman,* and the "radiance" or *claritas* of which he writes as being the occasion of esthetic arrest is *sānta-rasa,* the "flavor, taste, or sentiment" of rest in the recognition of *brahman.* Moreover, no matter what the subject matter, when viewed with the eye of vision cleared of deluding desires and fears, this recognition of the radiance will occur. For again, as told in the Gītā: "Whether upon a brahmin graced with learning and humility, a cow, an elephant, dog, or even an eater of dogs, the enlightened will look with equal eye."[33]

The way of the mystic and the way of the artist are related, except that (like Hairy, in the legend of "The Humbling of Indra") the mystic may come to regard the world with indifference, or even disdain. In the literature of asceticism passages abound of disparagement of the body, its functions and its motivations. A leading disciple of Ramakrishna, Swami Vivekananda (1863–1902), when on the point of death was heard to mutter, "I spit out the body." Whereas the artist who has been held by his craft in love to the world *as it is,* regarding with equal eye the brahmin, the dog, the eater of dogs, the slayer and the slain, cannot but recognize in each— whether in fascinated esthetic arrest, in pity (shared suffering), or sheer terror—something of himself. As Nathaniel Hawthorne declares in his short story, "Fancy's Show Box," telling of what dreams and fancies show of the innermost truth of each: "Man shall not disclaim his brotherhood, even with the guiltiest."[34]

There have been lately, however, a number of Western artists who have found such indifference to social evaluations reprehensible. I think, for example, of Thomas Mann, who, both in *Doctor Faustus* and in *Felix Krull,* two major works of his later years, describes the professional artist as a morally suspect, even socially dangerous, con man, who from a deliberately chosen position of spiritual alienation, yet offers the ambiguous, self-serving products of his art, in expectation not only of support and remuneration, but also of social approval and even adoration as a genius. Mann's argument here follows and develops that of Nietzsche *contra* Wagner;[35] also, Freud's psychoanalytic interpretation of art as a pathological symptom. In Freud's own words:

> There is a means of return from fantasy to reality, and that is art. To begin with, the artist is an introvert, almost a neurotic. Constrained by abnormally strong impulses, he desires honor, power, wealth, fame, and the love of women; but he lacks the means to attain these satisfactions, and so, like any other unsatisfied person, turns away from reality and transfers all of his interest, together with his libido, to the wishful fantasies of his imagination, through which he may be carried actually to neurosis. Several factors must coincide if he is not to follow this course to its conclusion. In fact, it is well known how frequently artists suffer partial impairment of their powers through neurotic applications. Their constitution probably includes a strong capacity for sublimation along with a certain degree of laxity in the repressions decisive for a conflict. The artist finds the road back to reality, however, in the following way.
>
> He is, of course, not the only one living a life of fantasy. The realm of fantasy is in fact a generally patronized resort, to which every sufferer from disappointments turns for refreshment and consolation. Those who are not artists are extremely limited, however, in their ability to derive pleasure from the wells of fantasy. The ruthlessness of their repressions compels them to make do with whatever meager daydreams they may dare to allow to become conscious. The genuine artist has more at his disposal. In the first place, he knows how to rework his daydreams in such a way that everything too personal, such as others might find offensive, is eliminated, and they become thus generally enjoyable. He knows, also, how to modify them, so that their origin in the forbidden wells is not immediately betrayed. And he possesses, further, the mysterious ability to shape some particular

material into a likeness of the model drawn from his fantasy. And finally, he knows how to render so much pleasure through these figurations from his unconscious that repressions are for the moment overcome and dispelled. The one who can achieve all this, thus making it possible for others to derive again refreshment and consolation from those wellsprings of their own unconscious which had become for them inaccessible, gains their thanks and admiration, and he has thus won through his fantasy what he had originally achieved only in his fantasy; namely, honor, power, and the love of women.[36]

The question finally at issue, however, is not of individual psychology, alienation, and resentment, but of the irreducible conflict of metaphysics *vis-à-vis* morals within the jurisdiction, not only of art, but of myth, religion, and social action as well. For during the course of the nineteenth century, the separation of these two opposed orders of human experience, concern, and fulfillment became in the West exaggerated to such a degree by the radical materialism of the increasingly industrialized megalopolitan centers of mass intelligence and democratization, that anything like the functional grounding of a social order in a mythology (so that individuals of whatever social class, participating in the metaphorical festivals, should become joined with all in a profoundly shared experience of the ground and sense of their lives) simply disappeared into irrelevance. And with that, the proper artist lost his public function. Today's pitiful contracts to invent monuments commemorating local-historical events and personages are hardly comparable to the earlier challenges of art, to break windows through the walls of the culture to eternity. Thus, the only true service of a proper artist today will have to be to individuals: reattuning them to forgotten archetypes, *les grandes lignes de la nature,* which have been lost to view behind a cloud of contending Jeremy Benthamoid philosophies of the "greatest [economic] good of the greatest number."

Thomas Mann, himself, in his early novelette *Tonio Kröger* (published 1903, when Joyce was at work on *A Portrait of the Artist As a Young Man),* described the quandary of a late-nineteenth-century young artist striving to find his way in art between the apparently contrary claims of morality and metaphysics, or as Mann termed them, nature and spirit. His title character, Tonio, having joined for a time an intensely intellectual company of bohemians in Munich, presently found their assumed superiority to the rest of mankind intolerable and, deserting them, mailed back an elaborate letter in which the nuclear idea was announced of an esthetic theory that became, in fact, the motivating inspiration of the art of Thomas Mann to the end of his career.

"I marvel at those cold, proud beings," Tonio wrote, "who adventure the ways of demonic, grandiose beauty and despise 'mankind.' But I do not envy them. For if there is anything that can make of a literary man a poet, surely it is this, my home-town love for the human, the living, and the ordinary. All warmth derives from this love, all kindness and all humor. Indeed, to me it even seems that this must be that love of which it is written that one may speak with the tongues of men and of angels, yet lacking it, be as sounding brass and tinkling cymbals."[37]

Some twenty years later, in response to a criticism of the apparent cruelty of his own verbal characterizations, Mann elucidated further what he had begun to call the "erotic" or "plastic irony" of his art: its dual loyalty to nature and to the spirit, to love and to truth. And here, in defense of himself, he came very close indeed to justifying in psychological terms the very qualities that in his novelette he had condemned and which in his later years he would again condemn. "The right word wounds," he wrote:

> The only weapon that has been given the sensibility of the artist, with which to react on appearances and experiences, defending him in the way of beauty, is this, of expressed delineation: which reaction (to use a radically psychological turn of speech) affords him a sublime *revenge* on the experience; the more vehement, the more refined the sensibility touched by the observation. Here is the source of that cold, inexorable precision in designation; here, the quivering, drawn bow from which the *word* flies—the sharp, feathered word, which hums and strikes and sits trembling on its mark.
>
> For is not the stem bow, as well as the gentle lyre, an instrument of Apollo? Nothing could be further removed from the truth of art than the notion that coldness and passion exclude each other: no misunderstanding greater, than to conclude from the critical accuracy of a statement that its inspiration, in the human sense, was of hostility and malice.[38]

"All life is sorrowful!" Thus the First Noble Truth of the Buddha. The aim of the quivering, drawn bow, therefore, the intended target of the feathered word, is but one feature of a context in which the artist himself participates, and the force that carries the arrow to its mark is compassion. The arrow, furthermore, is not the artist's own, but a gift to him, of which he is the responsible agent, a gift to him of the spirit, which is in love with the productions of time.

"The poet," Mann wrote, continuing his argument, "who does not offer himself up entirely is a useless drudge. . . . But how can I offer myself without at the same time giving up the world, which is my 'idea' *(meine Vorstellung),* my way of knowing, my agony, my dream?"[39]

During the years of the nightmare of the "war to end wars," World War I, while Joyce was at work in peace in Switzerland on *Ulysses,* Mann was laboring within beleaguered Germany on a volume of soul-searching political ruminations, *Betrachtungen eines Unpolitischen* ("Observations of a Nonpolitical Man"),[40] wherein the most conscientious analyses were undertaken of the relative values for humanity of those same contending monster-states that were then sacrificing to their common God the youth, the manhood, and the civilization of the Continent. Instead of disengaging his mind from judgment and regarding with equal eye the brahmin, the cow, the dog, and the eater of dogs, Thomas Mann, as a "Good European," was applying his whole soul to a thoroughgoing examination of the contemporary European conscience. Whereas Joyce, already in *A Portrait of the Artist As a Young Man,* had cut himself off completely from the values of his culture. *"Non serviam,"* he had quoted proudly, using a phrase attributed to Lucifer in his defiance of God, his Creator. "I will not serve that in which I no longer believe, whether it call itself my home, my fatherland, or my church."[41]

Moreover, compassion, as we learn from *The Tibetan Book of the Dead,* is of two orders: compassion with, and compassion without attachment.[42] The latter is of the Buddha and conduces to enlightenment, whereas the former leads to rebirth among the Hungry Ghosts.

For the judgmental (didactic) eye, whether of negation or of participation, is governed by a very different order of shared suffering and love than the eye at the top of the pyramid, which is of God (see pages 95–97), the God that is without and within; for whom, as we hear from Heraclitus

(c. 540–480 B.C.), "all things are fair and good and right; but men hold some things wrong and some right."[43] "Judge not, that you may not be judged," we are cautioned in the Gospels (Matthew 7:11; Luke 6:37); and again, in St. Paul's letter to his congregation in Rome: "God has consigned all men to disobedience, that he may have mercy upon all" (Romans 11:32).

James Joyce in *Finnegans Wake* made this last statement the motto of his novel, seeding through every chapter of the enigmatic book covert references to Paul's paradox by repeating ad infinitum, through innumerable transformations, the clewing number, 1132:[44] as a date (pages 13, 14, 119, and 420), the time of day (page 70), as the number of a legal document (page 61), of a musical composition (page 73), a street address (page 274), a registered patent (page 310), and so on and on and on *(passim),* giving point to this unrelenting reference to the spiritual message by casting as the leading character of the culminating masterwork of his life, upon which he labored for no less than eighteen years (1922–1939), a Dublin Englishman of the heritage of Cromwell.

"To my soul's satisfaction," Mann wrote in his scrupulous journal of World War I, "I find nothing in German history to compare with England's treatment of Ireland."[45] Economic and military imperialism, colonialism, and hypocritical democracy through centuries, Mann identified as the legacy of Great Britain, with the USA on the same course. Yet, twenty years later, in a political tract composed while touring the United States to urge this country into World War II: "Can it be denied," Mann asked rhetorically, "that the world, in so far as it is English, finds itself in right good hands?"[46] Ironically, a leading American author, Ezra Pound, was at that time in Italy, broadcasting condemnations of the Western Alliance that were very much like those of Mann's World War I *Betrachtungen.* Strindberg, I believe it was, who once said: "Politicians are one-eyed cats." The right eye, the left eye. Or one can close first one, then the other eye.

But the artist sees with two eyes, and alone to him is the center revealed: that still point, as Eliot saw, where the dance is. "And there is only the dance."[47]

So that, finally, it must be asked: "How far does one's mercy reach" (Romans 11:32)? For only so far do the inner and the outer worlds meet. And just so far is the reach of one's art. As the Californian, Robinson Jeffers, states in his poem "Natural Music":

The old voice of the ocean, the bird-chatter of little rivers,
(Winter has given them gold for silver
To stain their water and bladed green for brown to line their banks)
From different throats intone one language.
So I believe if we were strong enough to listen without
Divisions of desire and terror
To the storm of the sick nations, the rage of the hunger-smitten
    cities,
Those voices also would be found
Clean as a child's; or like some girl's breathing who dances alone
By the ocean shore, dreaming of lovers. [48]

CHAPTER NOTES

Introduction

1. For Spengler's vision of the Russian destiny, see *Der Untergang des Abendlandes,* 2 vols. (Munich: C. H. Beck'sche Verlagsbuchhandlung, 1918–1922), vol. 2, pp. 231–237. The *Decline of the West,* trans. by Charles Francis Atkinson (New York: Knopf, 1926–1928), vol. 2, pp. 192–196. "Pseudomorph," a mineral having the outward form of another species; in Spengler's sense, a culture expressed through the forms of an alien tradition: for example, Arabian culture in the first centuries A.D. under the forms of Rome.

2. Adolf E. Jensen, *Über das Töten als Kulturgeschichtliche Erscheinung,* in Jensen (ed.), *Mythe, Mensch und Umwelt* (Bamberg: Bamberger Verlagshaus Meisenbach, 1950; reprint. New York: Arno Press, 1978), pp. 24, 37.

3. W. B. Yeats, *The Collected Poems of W. B. Yeats,* "The Second Coming" (New York: Macmillan, 1966), pp. 184–185.

4. *Kena Upaniṣad* 29.

5. *Chhāndogya Upaniṣad* 24–25.

6. William Blake, "The Marriage of Heaven and Hell," with an introduction

and commentary by Sir Geoffrey Keynes (London/New York: Oxford University Press, 1975), p. 197.

7. Ananda K. Coomaraswamy, "The Vedanta and Western Tradition," in Roger Lipsey (ed.), *Coomaraswamy*, 3 vols. Bollingen Series LXXXIX (Princeton, N.J.: Princeton University Press, 1977), vol. 2, pp. 6–7; citing Walt Whitman, "Song of Myself," part 17, line 1, in *Leaves of Grass.*

8. *Kena Upaniṣad* 1.3 and 2.5. Italics and translation, mine.

9. James Joyce, *Finnegans Wake* (London: Faber and Faber; New York: Viking, 1939), p. 455, line 26.

10. Yeats, op. cit., p. 185, conclusion.

CHAPTER I

1. Immanuel Kant, *Prolegomena zu einer jeden künftigen Metaphysik, die als Wissenschaft wird auftreten können,* par. 36–38.

2. This creative *point* corresponds in sense and function precisely to the Indian *bindu* ("drop") out of which the original sound, *nāda* "shouted forth the universe."

3. Plato, *Timaeus,* 90d.

4. Ananda K. Coomaraswamy, "The Part of Art in Indian Life," in Roger Lipsey (ed.), *Coomaraswamy,* 3 vols. Bollingen Series LXXXIX (Princeton, N.J.: Princeton University Press, 1977), vol. 1, pp. 71 ff.

5. Plotinus II.9.16, cited and translated by Coomaraswamy, "Samvega: Aesthetic Shock," in Lipsey (ed.), op. cit., p. 185, n. 10, addendum.

6. John G. Neihardt, *Black Elk Speaks* (Lincoln, Neb.: University of Nebraska Press, 1968), pp. 20–47.

7. Ibid., footnote.

8. "Grimnismal," 23; Henry Adams Bellows, trans., *The Poetic Edda* (New York: The American-Scandinavian Foundation; London: Oxford University Press, 1923), p. 93.

9. Julius Oppert, "Die Daten der Genesis," *Abhandlungen der Königlichen Gesellschaft der Wissenschaften zu Göttingen.* Nachrichten, no. 10 (May 1877), pp. 201–223.

10. Kenneth H. Cooper, M.D., M.P.H., *Aerobics* (New York: Bantam, 1968), p. 101.

11. See Theodore H. Gaster, *The Dead Sea Scriptures in English Translation* (Garden City, N.Y.: Doubleday, 1956), pp. 281–306.

12. *The Book of the Twenty-four Philosophers (Liber XXIV philosophorum)*, in *Abhandlungen aus dem Gebiete der Philosophie und ihrer Geschichte. Festgabe zum 70. Geburtstag Georg Freiherrn von Hertling* (Freiburg im Breisgau: Herdersche Verlagshandlung, 1913), p. 13.

13. Friedrich Nietzsche, *Der Wille zur Macht* (1901), par. 223.

14. James Joyce in *Finnegans Wake* gives Anna Livia Plurabelle, the heroine of his dream book, the same polymorphous character, introducing throughout detectable references to her Hindu prototype, while casting H. C. E., her snoring spouse, in the role of Viṣṇu.

15. *Brahmavaivarta Purāṇa,* Kṛṣṇ-janma Khanda, 47.50–154. Translation following Heinrich Zimmer, *Myths and Symbols in Indian Art and Civilization,* edited by Joseph Campbell, Bollingen Series VI (New York: Pantheon, 1946; Princeton, N.J.: Princeton University Press, 1972), pp. 3–11.

CHAPTER 2

1. *Chhāndogya Upaniṣad* 8.3.2.

2. Immanuel Kant, op. cit., par. 58, footnote 2.

3. See the discussion of the relationship of this Kantian formula to the interpretation and evaluation of aboriginal myths and tales in my book, *The Flight of the Wild Gander* (New York: Viking, 1969), Chapter III, "Primitive Man as Metaphysician." The chapter was first published as a contribution to a volume honoring Paul Radin: Stanley Diamond, (ed.), *Culture in History* (New York: Columbia University Press, 1960).

4. See W. B. Yeats, *A Vision* (New York: Macmillan, 1925, 1938, 1956, 1961).

5. *Chhāndogya Upaniṣad* 9.4. and passim.

6. *The Gospel According to Thomas,* Coptic text, established and translated by A. Guillaumont, H.-Ch. Puech, G. Quispel, W. Till, and Yassah´abd al Masih (Leiden: E. J. Brill; New York: Harper, 1959), p. 43.

7. Ibid., p. 57.

8. Einar Pálsson, *Hypothesis As a Tool in Mythology* (Reykjavík: Mímir, 1984).

9. Ananda K. Coomaraswamy, The *Ṛg Veda As Land-Náma Bók* (London: Luzak, 1935), p. 34, n. 37.

10. The classic exposition in English is by Arthur Avalon (Sir John Woodroffe), *The Serpent Power* (Madras: Ganesh & Co.; London: Luzak, 1913, 3rd rev. ed., 1931).

11. Franz Pfeiffer *Meister Eckhart* (1857), trans. C. de B. Evans, 2 vols. (London: John W. Watkins, 1947), vol. 1, Sermon XCVI, p. 239. It should be added, perhaps, that twenty-eight of Eckhart's theological propositions were condemned by Pope John XXII.

12. *The Gospel of Sri Ramakrishna,* trans. with a preface, Swami Nikhilananda (New York: Ramakrishna-Vivekananda Center, 1942), p. 355.

13. Dante Alighieri, *The Divine Comedy,* trans. Charles S. Singleton, 6 vols. Bollingen Series LXXX (Princeton, N.J.: Princeton University Press, 1975): *Paradiso,* Canto XXXIII, lines 114–141, vol. 3, part 1, pp. 378–381.

14. *Ramakrishna,* op. cit., p. 355

15. Ibid., p. 858.

16. Ibid., p. 859.

17. Ibid., p. 103.

18. Philippians 2:8. *The Holy Bible: New Testament,* Revised Standard Version. The inserted reading, "clung to," is from *The Jerusalem Bible* (Garden City, N.Y.: Doubleday, Imprimatur, 1966).

19. Avalon, op. cit., pp. 108–114.

20. Avalon, op. cit., pp. 228–230.

21. *Ramakrishna,* op. cit., pp. 829–830.

22. Dante Alighieri, op. cit., *Inferno,* Canto XXXIV, lines 28–51, vol. 1, part 1, p. 363.

23. *The Gospel According to Thomas,* op. cit., pp. 3, 57.

24. James George Frazer, *The Golden Bough* (1890; reissued in 12 vols., 1907–1915), 1 vol. ed. (New York: Macmillan, 1922), p. 386.

25. *The Book of the Dead of Kenna* (19th dynasty from Thebes). Nederlandsches Museum van Oudheden te Leyden. C. Leemans, *Ägyptische Hieroglyphische Lijkpapyrus,* T. 2, *van het Nederlandsche Museum van Oudheden te Leyden,* Leyden, 1882. Also, Hannelore

Kischkewitz and Werner Forman, *Egyptian Drawings* (London: Octopus Books, 1972), plate 42.

I owe the discovery of this remarkable scene to the artist, Mark Hasselriis, and the identification of its source to the kindness of Professor Richard Smith, Fuller Theological Seminary, Pasadena.

26. *The Horizon Book of the Arts of China* (New York: American Heritage, 1969), p. 52.

27. Françoise Henry, *Irish Art during the Viking Invasions* (Ithaca, N.Y.: Cornell University Press, 1967), plate 80.

28. Eleanor Hull, *Early Christian Ireland* (London: David Nutt, 1905), pp. 150–161.

29. Avalon, op. cit., p. 215.

30. Daisetz T. Suzuki, "The Role of Nature in Zen Buddhism," in Olga Fröbe-Kapteyn (ed.), *Mensch und Erde*. Eranos-Jahrbuch, vol. XXII (1953) (Zurich: Rhein-Verlag, 1954), pp. 294–295.

31. Jeff King and Maud Oakes, edited with a commentary by Joseph Campbell, *Where the Two Came to Their Father: A Navaho War Ceremonial* (Bollingen Series I, 1943; New York: Pantheon, 1943; 2nd ed., Princeton, N.J.: Princeton University Press, 1969), p. 8.

32. *Altar of the Caduceus,* A.D. 15th century. *Codex Fejérváry-Mayer,* fol. 27. Merseyside County Museums, Liverpool, England.

33. R. Gordon Wasson, Albert Hofmann, and Carl A. P. Ruck, *The Road to Eleusis: Unveiling the Secret of the Mysteries* (New York: Harcourt, Brace, Jovanovich, 1978).

34. R. G. Wasson, *Soma: Divine Mushroom of Immortality* (New York: Harcourt, Brace, 1968).

35. Sylvanus Griswald Morley, *The Ancient Maya* (Stanford, Calif.: Stanford University Press; London: Oxford University Press, 1946), pp. 43, 284.

36. Heinrich Zimmer, op. cit., p. 15.

37. Verse from "The Blessing Chant," cited by Margaret Schevill Link, *The Pollen Path* (Stanford, Calif.: Stanford University Press, 1956), title page.

38. Jeff King and Maud Oakes, op. cit.

39. *Ramakrishna,* op. cit., pp. 362–363.

40. Ibid., p. 374.

41. Ibid., p. 830.

42. Gladys A. Reichard, *Navaho Religion: A Study of Symbolism,* 2 vols., Bollingen Series XVIII (New York: Pantheon, 1950), vol. 2, p. 390.

43. Ibid., vol. 1, p. 194.

44. Ibid., vol. 1, p. 193.

45. Ibid., vol. 1, pp, 197–200.

46. Ibid., vol. 1, pp. 190–192.

47. Ibid., vol. 1, p. 191.

48. Ibid., vol. 1, p. 192.

49. *Where the Two Came to Their Father: A Navaho War Ceremonial,* text and paintings recorded by Maud Oakes, given by Jeff King, commentary and introduction by Joseph Campbell, Bollingen Series I (New York: Pantheon, 1943; Princeton, N.J.: Princeton University Press, 1969).

50. Mircea Eliade, *Shamanism: Archaic Techniques of Ecstasy,* Bollingen Series LXXVI (New York: Pantheon, 1964), p. xvii.

51. *The Gospel According to Thomas,* op. cit., p. 55.

52. Avalon, op. cit., pp. 21–22.

53. *Ramakrishna,* op. cit., p. 355.

54. *Aṣṭāvakra Samhita* 6.1.

55. Dante Alighieri, op. cit., *Paradiso,* Canto XXX, lines 100–108, vol. 3, part 1, p. 341.

56. Ibid., Canto XXXI, lines 1–18, p. 347.

57. Dante Alighieri, op. cit., *Inferno,* Canto XXXIV, lines 37–45, vol. 1, part 1, p. 363.

58. *Hovamal,* 139–143; Bellows, op. cit., pp. 60–61.

59. *Grimnismal,* 31–32; ibid., p. 97.

60. *The Gospel According to Thomas,* op. cit., p. 25.

61. *Vivekacūḍamaṇi* 544–545.

62. Avalon, op. cit., pp. 290–291.

63. *Aṣṭāvakra Samhita* 15.6.

64. Natalie Curtis, *The Indians' Book* (New York/London: Harper and Brothers, 1907), pp. 349–350.

65. Ibid., p. 352.

66. Ibid., pp. 355–356.

67. Ibid., p. 349.

68. *The Gospel According to Thomas,* op. cit., p. 3.
69. Ibid., p. 43.
70. Ibid., p. 55.
71. *Vivekacūḍamaṇi* 516.
72. *Aṣṭāvakra Samhita* 1.16.
73. Arthur Schopenhauer, *"Transcendente Spekulation über die anscheinende Absichtlichkeit im Schicksale des Individuums,"* *Parera und Paralipomena,* I. Teil, *Sämtliche Werke,* 12 vols. (Stuttgart: Verlag der Cotta'schen Buchhandlung, 1895–1898), vol. 8, pp. 205 ff.
74. Ibid., p. 221.
75. Ibid., pp. 224–225.
76. Junjiro Takakusu, *The Essentials of Buddhist Philosophy* (Honolulu: University of Hawaii Press, 1947, 2nd. ed., 1949), p. 114.
77. Arthur Schopenhauer, *"Die beiden Grundproblemen der Ethik,"* II. *"Über das Fundament der Moral"* (1840), op. cit., vol. 7, pp. 253–254.
78. Ibid., p. 293.
79. Ibid., p. 254.
80. Ibid., p. 293.
81. Johann Wolfgang von Goethe, *Faust* II.5. 12104–12105.
82. Friedrich Nietzsche.
83. *Kena Upaniṣad* 2.3.

CHAPTER 3

1. *Brahmavaivarta Purāṇa.* Kṛṣṇa-janma Khanda 47.154–161.
2. See for this identification, Alain Daniélou, *Shiva et Dionysos* (Paris: Librairie Artheme Fayard, 1979), Engl. trans., *Shiva and Dionysus* (New York: Inner Traditions International, 1984).
3. James Joyce, *A Portrait of the Artist As a Young Man* (London: Jonathan Cape, Ltd., 1916), p. 211.; Viking Compass Edition, p. 207. The quotation is from *Summa Theologica* 1.5.4 AD. 1.
4. Friedrich Nietzsche, *Nietzsche contra Wagner,* *"Wo ich Einwände mache."*
5. Friedrich Nietzsche, *Der Wille zur Macht,* par. 808.
6. *Webster's New International Dictionary of the English Language*

(Springfield, Mass.: G. & C. Merriam, 1937), p. 2511, item "sublime," n.

7. Friedrich Nietzsche, *Der Wille zur Macht,* par. 853.

8. Joyce, op. cit., p. 235 (Viking Compass Edition, p. 207).

9. Ibid., p. 233.

10. Neihardt, op. cit., p. 47.

11. "The Marriage of Heaven and Hell," in Keynes (ed.), op. cit., p. 197.

12. Joyce, op. cit., p. 241 (Viking Compass Edition, p. 212).

13. Ibid., p. 241.

14. Ibid.

15. Ibid., pp. 242–243 (Viking Compass Edition, pp. 212–213).

16. Ibid., pp. 232–233 (Viking Compass Edition, p. 204).

17. Aristotle, *Poetics* VI.2.1449b.

18. Plato, *Laws* 840 c. See also, *Sophist* 226–227, *Phaedrus* 243 AB, *Phaedo* 66–67, *Republic* 399D.

19. *Webster's New International Dictionary,* op. cit.

20. Adapted and greatly abridged from *Jātaka* 1.68–71 and *Buddhacarita* 2–14.

21. T. S. Eliot, *Four Quartets,* "Burnt Norton" (San Diego/New York/ London: Harcourt Brace & World, 1943), pp. 15–16.

22. Joyce, op. cit., p. 242 (Viking Compass Edition, p. 213).

23. Coomaraswamy, "Art in Indian Life," in Lipsey (ed.), op. cit., pp. 90–91.

24. Heinrich Zimmer, *Artistic Form and Yoga in the Sacred Images of India,* trans. Gerald Chapple and James B. Lawson, with J. Michael McKnight (Princeton, N.J.: Princeton University Press, 1984), pp. 231–233; quotation from *Kulārnava Tantra* IX.44.

25. George C. O. Haas (ed. and trans.), *The Daśarūpa, A Treatise on Hindu Dramaturgy by Dhanaṃjaya* (New York: Columbia University Press, 1912).

26. *Daśarūpa* 1.6.

27. Ibid, 4.90.

28. Sir Monier-Williams, *A Sanskrit-English Dictionary* (Oxford: The Clarendon Press, 1888), p. 992, col. 3.

29. Joseph Campbell, *The Masks of God,* vol. 2. *Oriental Mythology* (New York: Viking, 1962; Penguin, 1976), pp. 325–327.

30. Johann Wolfgang von Goethe, *Sämtliche Werke, Jubiläumsausgabe*

(Stuttgart & Berlin: J. G. Cotta'sche Buchhandlung Nachfolger, 1902–1907), vol. 1. p. 258.

31. *Daśarūpa* 4.46.

32. *Bhagavad Gītā* 29–30.

33. Ibid., 5.18.

34. Nathaniel Hawthorne, "Fancy's Show Box," *Twice Told Tales* (1837, 1842).

35. Friedrich Nietzsche, *Nietzsche contra Wagner.*

36. Sigmund Freud, *Vorlesungen zur Einführung in die Psychoanalyse* (5. Auflage, 1926), pp. 390–391.

37. Thomas Mann, *Novellen,* 2 vols. (Berlin: S. Fischer Verlag, 1922), vol. 2, pp. 87–88. H. T. Lowe-Porter's translation of this passage will be found in Thomas Mann, *Stories of Three Decades* (New York: Knopf, 1936), p. 132.

38. Thomas Mann, *Rede und Antwort* (Berlin: S. Fischer Verlag, 1922), pp. 14–15.

39. Ibid., pp. 16–17.

40. Thomas Mann, *Betrachtungen eines Unpolitischen* (Berlin: S. Fischer Verlag, 1920), pp. 352–353.

41. Joyce, *A Portrait of the Artist As a Young Man,* op. cit., pp. 239, 247.

42. W. Y. Evans-Wentz, *The Tibetan Book of the Dead,* 3rd. ed. (New York: Oxford University Press, 1960).

43. Heraclitus, Fragment 102. From F. M. Comford, *Greek Religious Thought from Homer to the Age of Alexander* (London/Toronto: J. M. Dent and Sons; New York: E. P. Dutton, no date), p. 84.

44. All page numbers cited correspond to Joyce, *Finnegans Wake,* already cited, Introduction, n. 9.

45. Mann, *Betrachtungen eines Unpolitischen,* op. cit., pp. 352–353.

46. Thomas Mann, *This War* (New York: Knopf, 1940), p. 41.

47. T. S. Eliot, op. cit., pp. 15–16.

48. Robinson Jeffers, *Roan Stallion, Tamar, and Other Poems* (New York: Boni & Liveright, 1925), p. 232.

A JOSEPH CAMPBELL BIBLIOGRAPHY

Following are the major books authored and edited by Joseph Campbell. Each entry gives bibliographic data concerning the first edition. For information concerning all other editions, please refer to the mediagraphy on the Joseph Campbell Foundation website (www.jcf.org).

AUTHOR

Where the Two Came to their Father: A Navaho War Ceremonial Given by Jeff King. Bollingen Series I. With Maud Oakes and Jeff King. Richmond, Virginia: Old Dominion Foundation, 1943.

A Skeleton Key to Finnegans Wake. With Henry Morton Robinson. New York: Harcourt, Brace & Co., 1944.

The Hero with a Thousand Faces. Bollingen Series XVII. New York: Pantheon Books, 1949.

The Flight of the Wild Gander: Explorations in the Mythological Dimension. New York: Viking Press, 1969. *

The Masks of God, 4 vols. New York: Viking Press, 1959–1968. Vol. 1, *Primitive Mythology,* 1959. Vol. 2, *Oriental Mythology,* 1962. Vol. 3, *Occidental Mythology,* 1964. Vol. 4, *Creative Mythology,* 1968.

Myths to Live by. New York, Viking Press, 1972.

The Mythic Image. Bollingen Series C. Princeton: Princeton University Press, 1974.

Inner Reaches of Outer Space: Metaphor as Myth and as Religion. New York: Alfred van der Marck Editions, 1986. *

The Historical Atlas of World Mythology:

Vol. 1, *The Way of the Animal Powers.* New York: Alfred van der Marck Editions, 1983. Reprint in 2 pts. Part 1, *Mythologies of the Primitive Hunters and Gatherers.* New York: Alfred van der Marck Editions, 1988. Part 2, *Mythologies of the Great Hunt.* New York: Alfred van der Marck Editions, 1988.

Vol. 2, *The Way of the Seeded Earth,* 3 pts. Part 1, *The Sacrifice.* New York: Alfred van der Marck Editions, 1988. Part 2, *Mythologies of the Primitive Planters: The North Americas.* New York: Harper & Row Perennial Library, 1989. Part 3, *Mythologies of the Primitive Planters: The Middle and Southern Americas.* New York: Harper & Row Perennial Library, 1989.

The Power of Myth with Bill Moyers. With Bill Moyers. Ed. Betty Sue Flowers. New York: Doubleday, 1988.

Transformations of Myth through Time. New York: Harper and Row, 1990.

The Hero's Journey: Joseph Campbell on His Life and Work. Ed. Phil Cousineau. New York: Harper and Row, 1990.

Reflections on the Art of Living: A Joseph Campbell Companion. Ed. Diane K. Osbon. New York: HarperCollins, 1991.

Mythic Worlds, Modern Worlds: On the Art of James Joyce. Ed. Edmund L. Epstein. New York: HarperCollins, 1993.

Baksheesh and Brahman: Indian Journal 1954–1955. Eds. Robin and Stephen Larsen and Antony Van Couvering. New York: HarperCollins, 1995.

The Mythic Dimension: Selected Essays 1959–1987. Ed. Antony Van Couvering. New York: HarperCollins, 1997.

Thou Art That. Ed. Eugene Kennedy. Novato, California: New World Library, 2001. *

---

* Published by New World Library as part of the Collected Works of Joseph Campbell.

EDITOR

Books Edited and Completed from the Posthuma of Heinrich Zimmer:

Myths and Symbols in Indian Art and Civilization. Bollingen Series VI. New York: Pantheon, 1946.

The King and the Corpse. Bollingen Series XI. New York: Pantheon, 1948.

Philosophies of India. Bollingen Series XXVI. New York: Pantheon, 1951.

The Art of Indian Asia. Bollingen Series XXXIX, 2 vols. New York: Pantheon, 1955.

The Portable Arabian Nights. New York: Viking Press, 1951.

Papers from the Eranos Yearbooks. Bollingen Series XXX, 6 vols. Edited with R. F. C. Hull and Olga Froebe-Kapteyn, translated by Ralph Manheim. Princeton: Princeton University Press, 1954–1969.

Myth, Dreams and Religion: Eleven Visions of Connection. New York: E. P. Dutton, 1970.

The Portable Jung. By C. G. Jung. Translated by R. F. C. Hull. New York: Viking Press, 1971.

My Life and Lives. By Rato Khyongla Nawang Losang. New York: E. P. Dutton, 1977.

ACKNOWLEDGMENTS

Permission to quote extracts from the following sources is gratefully acknowledged:

Aerobics, by Kenneth H. Cooper, M.D., M.P.H. (New York: M. Evans and Company, Inc.). Copyright © 1968 by Kenneth H. Cooper and Kevin Brown. Reprinted by permission.

Artistic Form and Yoga in the Sacred Images of India, by Heinrich Zimmer, translated by Gerald Chapple and James B. Lawson with Michael McKnight (Princeton, N.J.: Princeton University Press). Copyright © 1984 by Princeton University Press. Reprinted by permission.

"Bilse und Ich," as translated by Joseph Campbell from *Rede und Antwort,* by Thomas Mann (Berlin: S. Fischer Verlag GmbH). Copyright © 1922 by S. Fischer Verlag GmbH. Used by permission.

Black Elk Speaks, by John G. Neihardt (Lincoln, Nebraska: University of Nebraska Press). Copyright © 1979 by the John G. Neihardt Trust. Reprinted by permission of Hilda Neihardt Petri for the John G. Neihardt Trust.

"Burnt Norton," in *Four Quartets,* by T. S. Eliot (New York: Harcourt Brace Jovanovich, Inc.). Copyright © 1943 by T. S. Eliot; renewed 1971 by Esme Valerie Eliot. Reprinted by permission.

Coomaraswamy, edited by Roger Lipsey, volume 1: *Selected Papers: Traditional Art*

INDEX

N

ABOUT THE AUTHOR

JOSEPH CAMPBELL was an American author and teacher best known for his work in the field of comparative mythology. He was born in New York City in 1904, and from early childhood he became interested in mythology. He loved to read books about American Indian cultures, and frequently visited the American Museum of Natural History in New York, where he was fascinated by the museum's collection of totem poles. Campbell was educated at Columbia University, where he specialized in medieval literature and, after earning a master's degree, continued his studies at universities in Paris and Munich. While abroad he was influenced by the art of Pablo Picasso and Henri Matisse, the novels of James Joyce and Thomas Mann, and the psychological studies of Sigmund Freud and Carl Jung. These encounters led to Campbell's theory that all myths and epics are linked in the human psyche, and that they are cultural manifestations of the universal need to explain social, cosmological, and spiritual realities.

After a period in California, where he encountered John Steinbeck and the biologist Ed Ricketts, he taught at the Canterbury School, and then, in 1934, joined the literature department at Sarah Lawrence College, a post he retained for many years. During the 1940s and '50s, he helped Swami

Nikhilananda to translate the *Upaniṣads* and *The Gospel of Sri Ramakrishna.* He also edited works by the German scholar Heinrich Zimmer on Indian art, myths, and philosophy. In 1944, with Henry Morton Robinson, Campbell published *A Skeleton Key to Finnegans Wake.* His first original work, *The Hero with a Thousand Faces,* came out in 1949 and was immediately well received; in time, it became acclaimed as a classic. In this study of the "myth of the hero," Campbell asserted that there is a single pattern of heroic journey and that all cultures share this essential pattern in their various heroic myths. In his book he also outlined the basic conditions, stages, and results of the archetypal hero's journey.

Joseph Campbell died in 1987. In 1988, a series of television interviews with Bill Moyers, *The Power of Myth,* introduced Campbell's views to millions of people.

THE JOSEPH CAMPBELL FOUNDATION (JCF) is a nonprofit corporation that continues the work of Joseph Campbell, exploring the fields of mythology and comparative religion. The Foundation is guided by three principal goals:

First, the Foundation preserves, protects, and perpetuates Campbell's pioneering work. This includes cataloging and archiving his works, developing new publications based on his works, directing the sale and distribution of his published works, protecting copyrights to his works, and increasing awareness of his works by making them available in digital formats on JCF's Web site.

Second, the Foundation promotes the study of mythology and comparative religion. This involves implementing and/or supporting diverse mythological education programs, supporting and/or sponsoring events designed to increase public awareness, donating Campbell's archived works (principally to the Joseph Campbell and Marija Gimbutas Archive and Library), and utilizing JCF's Web site as a forum for relevant cross-cultural dialogue.

Third, the Foundation helps individuals enrich their lives by participating in a series of programs, including our global, Internet-based

Associates program, our local international network of Mythological Roundtables, and our periodic Joseph Campbell related events and activities.

For more information on Joseph Campbell
and the Joseph Campbell Foundation, contact:

JOSEPH CAMPBELL FOUNDATION
www.jcf.org
Post Office Box 36
San Anselmo, CA 94979-0413
Toll free: (800) 330-MYTH
E-mail: info@jcf.org